I DROVE A RED CAR TO A BETTER ME

DEAN SKEWES

BALBOA.PRESS

A DIVISION OF HAY HOUSE

Balboa Press books may be ordered through booksellers or by contacting:

Balboa Press
A Division of Hay House
1663 Liberty Drive
Bloomington, IN 47403
www.balboapress.com.au
AU TFN: 1 800 844 925 (Toll Free inside Australia)
AU Local: 0283 107 086 (+61 2 8310 7086 from outside Australia)

Because of the dynamic nature of the Internet, any web addresses or
links contained in this book may have changed since publication and
may no longer be valid. The views expressed in this work are solely those
of the author and do not necessarily reflect the views of the publisher,
and the publisher hereby disclaims any responsibility for them.

The author of this book does not dispense medical advice or prescribe the use
of any technique as a form of treatment for physical, emotional, or medical
problems without the advice of a physician, either directly or indirectly. The
intent of the author is only to offer information of a general nature to help
you in your quest for emotional and spiritual well-being. In the event you use
any of the information in this book for yourself, which is your constitutional
right, the author and the publisher assume no responsibility for your actions.

Any people depicted in stock imagery provided by Getty Images are
models, and such images are being used for illustrative purposes only.
Certain stock imagery © Getty Images.

Print information available on the last page.

ISBN: 978-1-5043-2490-8 (sc)
ISBN: 978-1-5043-2489-2 (e)

Balboa Press rev. date: 03/16/2021

L ife unfolds before us, and our choices envelop us. For good or bad, our paths are redefined more often than we can imagine. Whether we choose to diverge from the road we are travelling and turn onto an obscure sidetrack or stick to the well-worn trail gouged out by the throng of the many before us, we are all ultimately in charge of our own journey and destiny.

Occasionally, though, we are denied the choice and are shunted onto a path we would never have taken. Our world is upended and turned inside out. We find ourselves at the mercy of events and outcomes beyond our control and circumstances we are ill-prepared to deal with.

More often than not in these situations, we are overwhelmed by the new norm we are forced to confront and are tested by the challenges laid before us. If we are very fortunate, we will have the love of a special person and the support of family and friends to help us deal with the challenges, to help us stand when we only have the strength to lie, to make us smile when tears flow freely, and to give us hope when there seems to be none.

This is my story of such a time. In the blink of an eye, I was cast adrift into an unfamiliar world to deal with all manner of challenges, testing my resolve and teaching me the importance of family and friends. I drove a red car to a better me, and I invite you to join me as I recall that journey. So put your seat belt on, and let's get going. Hold on tight—you know what they say about red cars!

I had lived a rather active life, but contrary to popular belief, being a shearer does not mean that you are a fit person. In fact, apart from upper-body strength and a flexible back, the constant bending seems to diminish your lung capacity. By the time I was forty, I was beginning to feel rather unhealthy. My diet did little to contribute to a healthy body. Quick, easy meals and a little too much alcohol had begun to take a toll on my well-being, so I bit the bullet and decided to get the train back on the tracks.

I began to jog and do stretches and lift some weights. As a result of this increased effort, I started to regain a little of my youthful strength and flexibility, and I also shed a few kilos of weight. The next ten years of work and play were a little easier. I had momentarily slowed the aging clock and was enjoying life to the full. I still enjoyed a few too many beers, but hey, you only live once!

By the time I was fifty, I was feeling bulletproof. I was running about twelve kilometres per week, and along with the weights and the like, I was feeling and looking pretty bloody good, and optimistically viewing the future.

I celebrated my fiftieth birthday in January 2013 and felt even happier when I caught up with my mates, a few of whom I had not seen for years. Most were younger than I. I was well and truly holding my own amongst the younger blokes. Fifty, bring it on. I couldn't have been more pleased and comfortable with my turnaround from ten years previous.

Contents

1. Our World as We Knew It

The bush ran deep and strong through our souls. Marise and I had both grown up on sheep properties in the New England area of New South Wales, twenty-five or so kilometres from each other. Our families had known each other for a hundred years at least. I am not implying that we were meant to be together, but that's how it turned out.

Marise's parents and mine socialised together in many community gatherings—tennis, cricket, dances, and so on—so we were familiar with each other, though not actually close friends. In our teens, the situation changed. In fact, it was a very complicated affair. Marise's older brother Garry and my younger sister Debbie began dating at about the same time as Marise and me. Garry and Debbie married in 1986, and then Marise and I in 1989. We settled on our respective family farms in due course, now seventeen kilometres apart.

Our families were very close by then, and our children grew up in a wonderful environment, surrounded by both sets of grandparents, a couple of great-grandmothers, a couple of great-grandfathers, and many cousins. I can't lie: there were times when constantly being so close to family was not easy. But in many ways, it was an ideal lifestyle, one our three daughters revelled in.

Marise and I were both passionate about animals and loved grazing sheep and a few cattle and living and working on the farm. We did have to work off-farm to supplement our incomes and build our family home, which involved me going shearing and Marise going wool-classing for many weeks of the year. But we loved where we lived and what we did together, and life was relatively grand.

Our girls attended Kingstown Public School, where Marise had schooled, a sixty-kilometre round trip every day. They then completed their secondary schooling at Uralla Central School, also where Marise had schooled, some sixty-five kilometres away.

By the time I turned fifty, well, the world was mostly rosy. Sarah was living with her partner, Mathew, and teaching at a primary school in Cessnock. Hannah was attending the University of New England in Armidale, training to be a PE teacher and living in Uralla with her partner, Jay. Zoe was in year 12 at Uralla Central and living with us at home. Marise and I were contemplating our next few years and pondering the prospects for our future. We were rolling, as always, with the variabilities of farming—droughts, floods, low commodity prices—as all farmers do. But all in all, we were comfortable, happy, and madly in love.

Marise and I had some pretty realistic plans for the next ten years. With Zoe now in year 12 and possibly off to university the following year, Marise and I would do a little more off-farm work and try to save enough money for a deposit on an investment house, maybe in Armidale, where Zoe could possibly live while at uni. We would have liked to put in a small pool, a double garage for storage, and a games room, setting up for a few years of fun and partying with our large family and friends.

★ ★ ★

In early 2013, we went through a nasty little drought on the farm, and so there was a little stress in our lives. We decided to take a few days' break and spend Easter with my youngest sister, Michelle, and her husband, Paul. Fine food and a few drinks would be just what the doctor ordered. Watch out, Brisbane!

We drove up to Brisbane on the Friday and settled in for a grand weekend. Michelle had everything organised. The beer flowed, and we relaxed, catching up on news and telling tales of our youth. Could it get any better? Our three beautiful daughters came with us. It was such fun, all being together for a long weekend. We were so fortunate. My mum and dad, Veronica and Noel, had also driven up for the weekend, so it was a real family weekend, one we had looked forward to for some time.

We had a lovely day Saturday. We drove out to a shopping centre on the north side of Brisbane in the morning and did a little shopping. Marise bought me a pair of those Croc sandals; she was a great fan of them and was sure I would enjoy them also. Back at Michelle's, we spent the afternoon helping her prepare for a little get-together with a few friends of hers. Dinner and some drinks? Well yes, don't mind if we do! We sat around that evening in the late autumn comfort that only Brisbane can offer, relaxing and chatting with our new friends.

One of Michelle's friends' husbands owned and operated a sign-making business and had recently completed a contract at Redcliffe, at a commemorative walkway for the Bee Gees. And as we were fans of their music and wondering what to do the next day, it was decided that we would drive up in the morning and take in the exhibit. We retired in the wee small hours after a wonderful evening to snare an hour or so of sleep before another fun-filled day.

★ ★ ★

Sunday morning, on reflection, was a rather disjointed affair. There was much discussion as to who would travel in which vehicle and who would sit where. Someone forgot her purse; someone wanted to be with us. We probably departed twenty minutes later than we anticipated. I was driving our red 2006 Falcon sedan. Marise was in the front with me; my brother-in-law Paul was in the passenger-side rear seat; and Sarah was in the driver-side rear. Michelle drove her Commodore station wagon. In with her were Dad, Mum, Hannah, and Zoe. It was very fortunate, I think, that there were five in their car and only four in ours.

Michelle and Paul lived in Tingalpa, so we headed east onto the Gateway Motorway and across the Gateway Bridge. Paul and I were discussing the development on the north shore of the Brisbane River as we crossed the bridge. He was working for Senator Ron Boswell at the time and had clear views on what was and what should be going on there. Michelle had been travelling behind us till the bridge, and thank God she passed us then, putting her in front of us on the freeway—just another good thing that happened that morning.

We were cruising along at about ninety-five kilometres per hour. The mood in the car was relaxed. There was not a lot of traffic on the road, maybe because it was about midday Sunday. It was very peaceful. We were very close to Nudgee, and I seem to recall that I had just passed a slower car, and as such we were in the right-hand lane when, out of the corner of my eye, I saw the shrubs in the median strip rustling.

It is amazing how fast the human brain can take in and analyse information, because although events obviously unfolded at breakneck speed, there are so many details that I can remember. The shrubs moving was peculiar, even at the time, because there was no wind. It was dead calm outside. There had not been a breeze to stir the trees along the freeway into motion, yet these shrubs, about three metres tall, were strangely moving.

Next, again so clearly, I saw something crash out of the scrub, maybe ten metres in front of us. It seemed to pounce, obviously because it was airborne and could have quite easily been a white tiger. I wish it had been in some ways. The white tiger—a very large tiger—was in fact a white car, and the realisation of this apparently caused me to say (and I have trouble writing this word so will use the more acceptable spelling), "F—k, hold on, I don't think we can miss it!"

I imagine half that sentence may have been uttered during the impact. I don't know how I could have said it in the little time I had between the realisation and the impact, and I do apologise sincerely to Marise, Sarah, and Paul for swearing every time the accident is mentioned.

I only recall one impact, but after the car had stopped spinning, we were hit by a car travelling behind us, which gave us another jolt. As for the first collision, I have no memory. More than likely, it happened so fast it was all over in a couple of seconds. There is a chance that I did lose consciousness, but if I did, it must have only been for a few seconds, because the creaking of metal, shattering of glass, and cloud of dust are still vividly etched into my memory.

Now, I honestly believe that at that very point, our bad luck finished, and things began to improve. Thankfully, I can say that now, as I did then, because of all the things that could have transpired in the immediate aftermath. Nothing bad happened, and as you will hear, there were plenty of opportunities for our situation to worsen.

When the car came to a stop, we were facing north, though diagonally across the right-hand lane. The car that had hit us was now behind us. I never saw it. I couldn't turn my body or head to look. Anything that did not occur in front of me from here on in, I never saw. I could only hear, and strangely, things were very quiet for a second or so.

My thoughts turned immediately to the others in the car, giving little thought to my own condition. Quite often in emergencies, we have the capacity to do the right thing, and I will be forever grateful that I was concerned with their plights before mine. I turned my head towards Marise, sitting in the passenger seat, her head slumped forward. There was blood coming from her mouth, and she wasn't moving at all. I'm sure my heart stopped. I was sure I had lost my dearest friend, my wife. In fact, in that split second, it occurred to me that I may have been inadvertently responsible for her death. In panic and desperation, willing her to be alive, I called to her.

"Marise, Marise, are you all right?" Half a dozen times I called to her. Then all of a sudden, her eyes slowly opened, and after a minute or so, although dazed and unaware of what had just happened, my dear wife nodded and said she was OK.

Next, I called to Paul, in the passenger side rear. He immediately replied that he was all right, though he was obviously dazed as well. I then enquired as to Sarah's condition. She was tearful and said she thought that her right arm was broken, which in fact it was, but she was fine enough. I then took stock of my own condition, seemingly from a third-person perspective. I managed to evaluate the situation quite rationally and somehow oblivious to the underlying pain now wracking my body.

I informed the others that I thought my left foot was broken. It was wedged between the brake pedal and the floor, and crushed by whatever else was down there, I tried to lift my right arm, which hung limp. It was broken, which I also relayed to them.

I then looked down at my right thigh. I was wearing my favourite shorts, a pair of orange Tangerine turtles. Their loss is still keenly felt. What a way for a pair of shorts to meet their end! But back to the story. My right thigh was badly broken, the bone protruding through the skin and the blood oozing from the wound—a dead giveaway.

I don't know why I didn't start swearing or crying. In fact, there are probably many acceptable things to do under similar circumstances. But I just methodically evaluated the situation and passed on my report to the others. Once I had informed them of my condition, I remember saying, "Well, if you are all relatively OK, I may just concentrate on my situation, if you don't mind," or something to that effect. A calmness quite unexpectedly came over me. I was obviously in shock, and I probably started drifting in and out of consciousness.

★ ★ ★

The dynamics of the following events are very intricate, and from here on, everyone's recollection is different. Where they were, and what they heard and saw, makes their individual story different from all others. It was months before we were able to get together and each tell our own story, which helped us all apply a more accurate storyline and timeframe to the events of that day.

Obviously, in the condition I was in, my recollection of events is likely to be muddled. Still, this is how I recall what occurred inside that crumpled vehicle that sunny morning. Each of us has a different memory as to the sequence of events, and that is entirely understandable. A lot happened very quickly, though it seemed to take hours.

Paul managed to get his door open and apparently assisted Sarah out of the car via his door. He then attempted to release Marise, but her door was damaged and could not be opened. Marise remained in the car beside me. It did comfort me to have her near, talking to me and helping me through the ordeal.

Some very kind people—they really were angels—pulled up immediately. They may have been the people in the car that clipped us. They had young children in their car, and they came to offer assistance in whatever form it could take. I think they had a blanket or some such that Sarah laid on, on the road, beside our car.

One of them sat behind me and held my head still and talked to me constantly, trying desperately to keep me conscious, until the ambulances arrived. The other held Marise's head still. I think they were husband and wife. I never saw their faces, but I will try to contact them soon to thank them dearly for the wonderful comfort and help they were to us both in our hour of need.

Paul, as I mentioned earlier, was working for Senator Ron Boswell and was immediately on his phone, not just calling the ambulance—he was talking to ministers, telling them to arrange a rescue helicopter or what they could quick smart. Paul did an awesome job. For the care he gave Sarah during all this, I will be eternally indebted and love this man forever.

Remembering the events of that day is still very emotional for me. I still get teary on recalling them. One point in particular pains me dearly. As I have said, Paul helped Sarah from the car and lay her on a blanket kindly lent by the people who were in the car with Marise and me. There was much concern in regard to the fluids seeping from the car, and there was fear that the fuel might ignite and the car catch alight.

Sarah was moved farther away. She was terrified, sure that the car would catch fire and she would lose her mum and dad, even though both of us had survived the immediate crash. I can only imagine the terror our dear girl experienced at that point. She was quite vocal in her desire to stay near and adamant that there would be no fire.

Sarah must suffer some long-term mental scarring as a result of that particular moment. I am sure that something as frightful would leave me scarred. I have never asked in relation to her feelings in regard to that particular point and must one day do so. Paul did a wonderful job of reassuring her that all would be fine. Sarah was eventually settled, somewhat, as events unfolded.

It seemed an eternity, for me in particular, and Marise says it was for her also. When Marise regained consciousness, as she recalls, I was full of apologies for having the accident, smashing our dear car to bits, and causing them such pain. I do not recall much of this, but I still hold myself responsible for the accident, inasmuch as I somehow believe I should have been able to avoid the other car. I know not how I could have done so. I recall veering to the left in an attempt to let the approaching car pass behind us, to no avail. I am mortified at the prospect that in my attempt to avoid the accident, the other car may have collided with our car, more towards the rear, and that Sarah may have taken the full impact. I dread the thought, so I am relieved that my attempt to save us from the crash was unsuccessful, in some respects.

The minutes ticked by. Marise's recollections are few. She recalls the couple holding our heads in spite of the fear of a fire, or worse an explosion, and she remembers the arrival of the ambulances and the rescue team. I must have been struggling to maintain consciousness. The gentleman holding my head worked on me continuously to stay awake.

When the ambulance arrived, we were obviously assessed, apparently sedated, and given something for the pain. I recall none of this. I do remember, though, the rescue team placing a sheet over us and breaking the windscreen, cutting the roof from the car, and cutting off the doors. All these procedures were quite noisy and disturbing, as our car was crunched, torn, and dismantled to facilitate our removal. Marise was released after the roof and her door were removed. My release took a little longer, as my left foot was trapped beneath the brake pedal.

★ ★ ★

It was from this point on that things became wacky for me, whether as a result of the sedatives or not. I will never be certain, but I had some funny thoughts. I have pondered on what I experienced, and wondered why I did so, ever since. I'll attempt to recall what transpired in my head. Well, it must have occurred in my head; there was nowhere else for it to have happened. It may have been a dream, but was I asleep? I imagine being asleep or being sedated require different states of consciousness. Which one it was, I'll never know. You'll just have to read on and make up your own mind.

The first thing I remember was an unconscious memory, but realistically vivid, and very real at the time. Now, I am far from a computer expert—actually, my understanding of computers and their programs is basic, to say the least—but somehow I was trapped in a computer program. I was lying on what seemed to be a table inside a computer, and I was being analysed. The program was analysing my entire life. It seemed as if my life was streaming by in many flashing lights and colours, careering at breakneck speed, and I was unable to move, talk, or have any influence on the process at all.

The program was accompanied by the most frightful screeching noise, louder than anything I could imagine, and I was dying. I knew I was dying. I was becoming weaker. I had little strength and couldn't bear the torture much longer. But still it went on.

It then dawned on me that maybe I was already dead, and this torture might last for eternity. I slumped even deeper into despair. I could feel myself letting go. If this was death, and if in fact I was already dead, I could not go through an eternity of this pain. I was crying in pain and despair. The situation was hopeless, and I could not conceive of a means of escape. Neither could I just let go. This might also be the last rites, so to speak. Maybe I would die soon, and this would all be over. If this was the case, then I was prepared to let go and, well, die! If I could just die and release myself from this torture, I would dearly exit stage right now.

At this point, virtually at wits' end and totally exhausted, a thought came to me and a glimmer of hope presented itself. From somewhere in my teenage memories—and this was without any doubt to me—I remembered a song. The words were so clear to me. It was as if I had known them and only them forever. I had a feeling that if I held tight to these words, repeating them over and over to myself, that maybe they would deliver me from this hell I now plunged through. I felt so weak but repeated the words over and over again, with all my might, hoping in vain that somehow it might help me.

I told myself that if I lived, if I managed to escape from this hell, I would never, ever forget that song—the song that could save my life. It was a song that I would not be able to recall by day's end. Maybe, in later years, in those final few moments of life, I will be reunited with that song. It has given me so many more glorious blessed years of life.

* * *

My next memory is of waking up, still in the car, but with a strange removed sense, and with the world rolling from top to bottom at a million miles an hour. The direction in which the car had come to rest had it pointing diagonally towards the timbered country on the western side of the freeway, so what I could see was the wrecked front of the car and the trees and vegetation before me. The scene was tumbling from top to bottom, extremely fast, but slowing always, till at last it was still, and I took in the vista in disbelief.

Before me was a world that I had never truly seen before. It was so bright and clear, and the colours were so vivid. The sky was blue as blue, and the foliage and everything was so crisp. The trees now rustled, and their branches swayed ever so dreamily. I felt such peace—a peace I had never experienced before—and a calmness. These were such a relief after the horrid computer program nightmare.

There now seemed a clarity to my world. Then maybe I was sedated again, for all was gone. I was obviously released from the car, placed in an ambulance, and whisked away to the Princess Alexandra Hospital in Brisbane. My first ambulance trip, and I do not remember a single second of it.

Marise and Paul were taken there also, in separate ambulances. Sadly, Sarah was taken to Redcliffe Hospital, where she would battle through her own torture over the next few days—another of the eventualities I hold myself responsible for. So much pain came from that accident. The driver of the car that hit us was taken to another hospital, I am unsure which one, with similar injuries to me, apparently. I had such sympathy for that poor man. It must have been unimaginable what he went through, at the time and ever since.

In my opinion, there were only victims of the accident. No one escaped unscathed, and finger-pointing achieves nothing. We all survived to deal with the aftermath in our own ways, and in our own good time, as fate would have it.

2. AND WHO WOULD HAVE THOUGHT THAT TERRORISTS WERE INVOLVED?

"I can't tell you anything, I don't know what you want with me. I have no idea who you are, where we are, or what is happening. Can you please let me go, please!"

I had been abducted by terrorists, and I was being held in a small, dingy room. I lay on a bed while the two men interrogating me hovered over me with intent—to torture, I suspected; to murder, I feared! God only knows why or how, but they had me, and whatever they wanted from me or imagined that I knew, well, all I could do was tell them over and over again that I couldn't help them. I didn't know anything! I couldn't move. My body was restrained, lashed to the crude bed.

They were unimpressed by my refusal to comply, and their actions became more menacing.

"Please, please, let me go, let me go!" I cried.

I tugged at the tube in my nose, trying to free myself from the discomfort it caused me, only to be told nicely by the nurse that I must leave it in. She then moistened my lips with some balm,

13

and I drifted off to sleep again. Thankfully, this time the terrorists had gone. They had probably jumped into the head of some other poor soul in the ward.

What a strange dream to have! It was one that I would ponder for some time. The list of perplexing issues arising as a result of the accident grew daily. I spent the first of April in intensive care, oblivious to the world and, thankfully, the pain.

★ ★ ★

The next memory I have was of watching Hannah, Zoe, Shelley, Mum, Dad, and Marise walking around the corner into the ward I had reawakened in. Dad was in a wheelchair—the first time I had seen him in one. The accident had really shaken him. He aged terribly over the next few months and only went downhill over the next few years. Another eventuality I feel I contributed to. So very sorry, dear man, so very sorry.

They all stood around the bed, chatting away. It was very tough for me. The morphine was not to my liking. I struggled with it, hating the fogginess of my mind and the constant sleepiness. I could not concentrate on anything for any time at all.

Sarah obviously wasn't with them, and it was terrible to hear that she was in Redcliffe Hospital and all alone. Paul and Michelle took it in turns of going up to see her, and bringing Marise and the girls in to see me. They filled me in on all that had occurred since the accident.

It is very strange to lose track of events. Quite often, when you travel, you awaken in a strange bed or environment, and it takes a minute or two to straighten things out in your head. Well, this was even more confusing, because the last real normal memory I had was of driving along the freeway. From first seeing the car approaching, all thoughts had been so disjointed and frantic, they had been lost. Well, not exactly *lost*, but catalogued somewhere, requiring further analysis, before I could fully understand them. From what I have heard, this is what happened.

On our arrival at the Princess Alexandra Hospital, Marise had been seen, x-rayed in an MRI, and admitted. She was terribly shaken, had cuts and bruises, and her hair and clothes were full of glass pieces. She was very uncomfortable for many days to come. Paul had been seen and was suffering from terrible bruising to his upper body from the seat belt, but he was released to go home. Marise would spend the night in hospital under observation.

The ambulance in which I was transferred had obviously been in contact with the hospital, informing them of my condition, so radiology had been told to power up the MRI in readiness for me. Michelle had followed the ambulance to the hospital, and Hannah and Zoe were allowed into the room I was in before I went to the MRI. They were shocked by my condition.

The doctor in charge asked them if I had been in a high-speed motorcycle accident, as the injuries were consistent with that. He was shocked to hear it had been a car accident; my injuries so severe. I was covered by a sheet, which the girls said was soaked in blood, and they could see the lump under the sheet where my broken femur was protruding. No doubt it was a traumatic experience for them both.

Sometime after my MRI, I was obviously taken to surgery, where I was put back together in a long, complex operation. My fractured femur was nailed—a procedure that involved a titanium nail, the length of my femur, being inserted down the inside of my femur after the bone was drilled out. My femur had also broken at its neck, where it joined the pelvis. It was secured with multiple screws. The ulna in my right forearm was plated. I had a broken left foot and a ruptured posterior medial ligament in my right knee. Both these injuries remained untreated; they would heal of their own accord, in time.

★ ★ ★

Eventually, I was transferred to intensive care. The surgeon had surely seen enough of me by this stage. The mood must have been sombre back at Michelle and Paul's that night, while I hung out in the hospital, sleeping soundly and oblivious to all.

A couple of days later, Zoe took photos of me and my wounds. I couldn't bring myself to look at them at that stage. It was months before I did. I wasn't strong enough emotionally to handle that aspect of the accident. Likewise, they had been to the facility where the car was taken to retrieve the things from the car. Zoe took photos of the car also, and likewise, it was many months before I could bring myself to look at them.

So there I lay in hospital. There were another three beds in the ward. It was a couple of days before I was strong enough to converse with any of my roommates, if you can call them that. There were two women and a young man. He had been in a car accident months before and had had an artificial knee implant at the time. Recently, he had fallen in the shower at home, and the bone around the implant had broken.

I felt sorry for him. He was so young, and it would have an impact on his entire life. He was so anxious about the outcome and relieved when it was decided that no further operation was required. But he would have to stay off the leg for another two months.

Across the room from me was a lady who was suffering from severe back pain but wasn't happy at all to be in hospital. One morning, while trying to get out of bed, she fell heavily to the floor. She had fainted and fallen. Somebody rang the assistance bell, and we waited for a couple of minutes for a nurse to come. We tried to talk to her, asking if she was all right, but she was still unconscious.

The nurses managed to return her to bed, and she was OK. That was a relief. We were afraid that she might have hurt her back even more, but it seemed not. A couple of days later, she was released, with no resolution of her complaint. Her pain had subsided, and she was well enough to return home.

I was struggling to get my head around my situation. I had never spent a night in hospital before. I had always feared a hospital stay. How would I put in the time? I would be so bored. But to my relief, I was so very weak, I couldn't imagine being anywhere else. I obviously had many broken bones, but bones heal, and even I knew about six to eight weeks healed most breaks. My reasoning was that after six to eight weeks, I would be fully recovered, up walking, back shearing, on with life. *So, let's recover. Don't want to put on too much weight, do we? So let's eat healthily.*

A couple of days down the track, I could tell that I needed more sustenance. My iron levels were very low, as I had lost so much blood. I needed food to build the levels up again. If my iron levels did not rise in a couple of days, I would need a blood transfusion. Blood samples were taken twice daily to access their levels. I was so weak, and there was no doubt in my mind, by now, that I needed to eat, and forget about the weight.

Marise fed me for the first week. I had little strength to lift my head. I was surprised that I was slowly getting weaker, not stronger, as my body began to lose muscle tone, which apparently happens after only about three days of inactivity. Meals were protracted events; with the weakness I felt and the tiredness, I often fell asleep while eating.

Marise was, as she continues to be, an absolute angel. I remember saying to her that if I was too much for her, I would understand if she had to leave me. This wasn't the gig she had signed up for when we had married. For better or worse didn't include this, I told her. She insisted that all was OK. All I needed to concern myself with was getting better, and however long it took, she would be there for me.

Marise's reassurance was the medicine I dearly needed, but the lingering suspicions I had about what the future might hold gave me endless concern. Would I ever again be the person I was, the fun-loving, have-a-go-at-anything larrikin? I feared not. Would I be able to manage the property and accomplish the farm work I so dearly loved? Would I ever be able to shear again? In essence, would I be me, or would I have to reinvent myself?

I soon broached the subject when all were at the hospital one day, laying the cards on the table and proclaiming that many stock would have to be sold, as we would be unable to manage them from now on. There would have to be more time for family. It was to become my priority—as I saw it, my second chance at life should not be wasted on work and more work. All were in agreement. I am sure they would have agreed to anything so as not to upset me at that stage. I have felt sorry since that I used my infirmity to push my ideas upon them. It was unnecessary at the time. I should have waited till things had settled down. As things panned out, eventually we were able to manage reasonably well, although things were never quite the same.

★ ★ ★

I had the obligatory morphine drip with a button to use when the pain was too intense. For a day or two, I used it often, but I soon realised that it was unnecessary. I gave it up and reverted to the Panadol that was regularly offered. I was still on Endone tablets, which I took for another day or so till I realised that they too were keeping me in a constant daze. Marise was with me all through the days, and I so wanted to be able to talk to her sensibly. She had also brought in some puzzle books, and we would do the crosswords together. I was of little help in my drugged state, but cutting down on the Endone slowly cleared my head a little.

It is hard to describe the weakness and tiredness I felt. Never had I felt as I did then. Closing my eyes to relax a little inevitably resulted in me falling asleep. For the first couple of days, each time I awoke from these sleeps, I was confused as to where I was. It was quite disturbing.

I have always been a light sleeper, but I could now sleep through the dramas of a hospital ward, at least during the day. The nights were a different matter. I would lay awake, conscious of every noise and movement, every buzzer, moan, cough, footstep. I watched television till the wee small hours, trying in vain to reach that point where you just fall off to sleep from sheer exhaustion, but I failed to reach it. I would only manage to nod off for ten minutes or so. I'd wake to look at the time on the TV and realise the futility of it all.

The nights were my hell. I feared them. I became ever so worked up about them, which made matters worse. For the first few days, the lack of night sleep made me more tired during the day, and so the night became even more of an ordeal.

After a few days, I asked the nurse if I could have sleeping tablets to help me. She saw the doctor, and they were prescribed. My prayers were answered. I would only have to ask the nurse on duty, and I would have my little peace of mind.

There was only one glitch to my plan for world domination: it seems that sleeping tablets work solidly on me for four hours max. After four hours of blissful, undisturbed slumber, my eyes shot open, and that was that. So taking the tablet at about eleven at night resulted in me, by three in the morning, lying in bed as alert as a meerkat. This then left me with two or so hours till the morning routine began—more boredom and frustration, tick, tick, tick!

The next night though, a slight change to the plan had me taking my tablet at about twelve thirty, the latest time they would allow me to take it. About four thirty sharp, eyes open, yawn, stretch, yes, this is about right, we can cope with this. Once again, meticulous planning and some minor adjustments had delivered the desired result. I could now manage the nights, and my hospital stay would be a more relaxing adventure.

I am delighted that I was able to use the word *meticulous* in the previous paragraph. Anyone who knows me will certainly not associate me in any way with *meticulous*, and in fact, I doubt if I have ever used the word in relation to anything I have ever done before or since. So there's one for me!

★ ★ ★

I must add at this point that I was still, obviously, rather immobile, mainly lying on my back, occasionally turning from side to side a little, and being held in place by many strategically placed pillows. Turning was a very painful affair, requiring the assistance of a couple of nurses and a wards-man. I was in such pain after these moves; it is hard to describe. I would need to just lay still and compose myself for ten minutes or so till the pain eased. I also had the mandatory catheter, which would invariably become caught during these movements and tear at my nether regions like all hell until placed in a comfortable position again.

Compression socks were a little uncomfortable in bed, but when they were coupled with the air-inflated socks that went on your feet and pumped up and released every thirty seconds or so to keep your circulation healthy, you could be sure you were having a real ball. I am sure the air-inflated ones were invented by the SS in World War II! I hung out like a junkie waiting for the times they would take the pumping things off and give me a break. The longer the break the better; I was in no hurry to be hooked up again and certainly didn't remind the nurses if they had been off for too long.

With cannulas and the constant needles, which I also had a real fear of before the accident, I was having a rather tough and uncomfortable time of it. The whole affair did cure me of my aversion to needles, however. I even managed to get to the stage where I would give myself the blood-thinning needles. This was a massive step for me and an added benefit of the ordeal.

So hospital life, once a foreign concept and a terrifying prospect, became a matter of careful planning and routine once I began to embrace it. My day started at four thirty when I awoke from my drug-induced slumber. There followed a blood pressure and temperature check, obligatory name and birthdate, Panadol, water, and associated housekeeping, including having my wee bottle emptied, tidying up my table from the night's medication containers and other pieces of rubbish, and preparing myself for the upcoming day.

★ ★ ★

In the bed beside me, by this stage, was a gentleman about my age who had finally made it into the wards after two months in intensive care. He had been riding his push bike with some friends out and about Toowoomba. They were on the highway. He was bringing up the rear of the group when he was hit by a semitrailer.

I mention Steve at this point because he was a real character when it came to the nurses asking him his name and birthdate. Steve would give his name and birthdate and then, when asked if he had any allergies, say he was allergic to penicillin, something else, and trucks! It still brings a smile to my face and makes me laugh to think of him saying that.

With all Steve had been through and was still going through, he retained that spark of humour. Laughter, though painful, did wonders for us both. We also had many deep and meaningful talks in the wee small hours, much needed by both of us, I must admit. We helped each other out on many occasions, particularly when one of us was feeling down.

One morning, as we went about our dailies, we were interrupted by the incessant and annoying clatter of the fire alarm. There was little concern shown by any nurses, and though some immediate alarm was voiced by the residents of the ward, we were reassured that an intermittent ringing presented no need for concern. We should only be concerned if the ring took on a continuous form.

Well, glory be, no sooner had the nurse eased our fears than the alarm *did* take on a continuous ring. The ward was enveloped in a mood of hysteria. Well, not quite, but there was obvious concern, particularly seeing that all of us were mobility challenged and, in fact, incapable of getting out of our beds.

There was now a poorly disguised fluster evident in the staff's behaviour, and we waited in trepidation as to the next move. A faint wafting scent of smoke now lingered in the room, and evacuation seemed in the cards. Luckily, the fire was contained in an electrical switchboard, and after a short time, it had been extinguished, and the threat to life and limb was averted. A collective sigh of relief emanated from the residents, and when our heart rates had dropped, normality, such as it was, returned to our little world. Our daily excitement had come and gone, and we had another little shared experience that all could chuckle about for the next few days.

★ ★ ★

So, back to the routine. Housekeeping done, the morning show on TV, and a cuppa and biscuit, then a little light reading ... well, not too light. It may have been Michelle who brought me a book to read. It sat on my table for a couple of days, staring at me, calling me, daring me to pick it up and taste it, and it eventually wore me down. I'd read very little since Marise and I were married—I'd not had the time or inclination—but now it seemed I had time, and possibly plenty of it.

So I took the book up one day, stared a young Bob Dylan in the face, and prepared myself to feast upon his early life. Reading gave me the means to occupy myself when Marise wasn't with me. I found that I really enjoyed it—the book, the process, the release from the present reality. It would inspire me to take reading up for relaxation once more, another significant benefit of the accident.

Breakfast was always welcome. Hmm, cornflakes, fruit and some yoghurt, yum, yum. So much nicer then plain old Weetabix and milk, a nice glass of juice, and sharp white coffee. Then the doctors would make their rounds, and Marise would arrive.

Next came the ritual washing—not laundry, me of course, a procedure that offered no terror to me at all. Coming from the cooler climes of New South Wales, I was finding the April weather of Queensland quite warm and balmy, so I chose to sleep naked, under one sheet with a fan blowing on me, which was kindly sourced by one of the many wonderful nurses. I had no qualms about my nudity, and being in such a vulnerable state, I gave up any concept of embarrassment I may have ever had. Whatever had to be done, I was by no means concerned, and gave up my modesty, making it as easy as possible for the nurses.

At one point only did a nurse object to my individual comfort. One elderly nurse, who was thankfully only on for one shift during my stay, insisted I wear a gown and be neatly wrapped up in the appropriate number of sheets and blankets, for my own good obviously, but also, apparently, for the good of the staff and other patients. There could be no exception to the rules; I must submit and comply.

I battled through the shift. The other nurses apologised and reassured me that on her finishing her shift, all would be returned to my liking. Was I being selfish, possibly? But I was so very easy to deal with. I never caused dramas, never abused the staff—in fact, I often put up with discomfort instead of bothering the nurses. I had little say in anything befalling me at the time; surely the desire for a little comfort was understandable.

★ ★ ★

After my daily sponge bath, I was left feeling quite fresh and clean. Bring on the physio! The physios would call before lunch, after my midmorning cuppa and biscuit. A couple of Panadols before they came would help me through their torture.

A couple of days into my stay, the physio decided I should get up and try to walk. Now, I still don't know whose brainwave this was, but they really needed to be called to account on this matter. I was far from ready for such frivolity; in fact, it was a month or so before I could finally stand with the aid of only a crutch. But there we were, the physio, a nurse, and me regaled in a moon boot on my left foot, a very weak and severely damaged right leg, a broken right ulna, and a set of crutches resting precariously against a chair. The physio and nurse—the latter obviously only following orders, which she more than likely believed foolish—managed to position me in a chair before the spectacular attempt, on a par with Hillary's ascent of Everest. With much help, I was stood upright and released.

The resulting fall—luckily backward and into the chair—was obviously noted with alarm by the physio. I was hurried back into bed. No further attempts were made in regard to standing or walking, by the physio or anyone else.

I was talking to a friend the other day. He had been in a horrific car accident, in which he suffered broken ribs, broken vertebrae, broken leg, and twenty-three breaks of his pelvis, as well as damage to the back of his hand. He had skin grafts to his hand injury, and this one day a young doctor had come to change the dressing on his hand injury.

When the doctor had finished, he said, "Well, there you are. You should be going home in a day or two."

He was totally oblivious to the associated injuries, and I think that is what happened in my case. The physio had noted I had a broken left foot, saw my arm in a cast, and thought, *Well, that is the extent of his injuries. Let's get him up and moving.* I think there would have been hell to pay if the surgeon had found out about the stupidity of the physio's actions. I never mentioned the incident, choosing not to cause dramas, but maybe I should have spoken up!

★ ★ ★

After the daily physio—far less aggressive after the previous visit—I would recover and then we would lunch. I realised quite quickly that my best option in regard to lunch was a sandwich, an option quickly taken up by Steve. It seemed that sandwiches were basically foolproof. It wasn't easy to ruin a chicken salad, or corn meat and tomato sandwich. Meanwhile, other items on the lunch menu were a little bit of a lucky dip in regard to what you imagined you were going to get and what actually turned up. Sandwiches got a thumbs-up from Steve and me.

After lunch, there was always a little nap. I had little trouble sleeping during the day; I have often wondered why. A little nap, taken while Marise went to the kiosk for her lunch, would refresh me for the afternoon. Marise would bring me back a coffee from the kiosk. Oh, the joy!

We would do puzzles. She would read magazines to me. We would chat and fill in the time till afternoon tea. More cuppa and biscuits, then winding down for the evening and dinner.

Michelle had taken a week off work after the accident to be with Mum and Dad. So she would bring Marise into the hospital in the mornings, and then Michelle and Paul would bring Mum and Dad in to see me of an evening before taking Marise home. When Michelle went back to work, Marise would get a lift to the hospital with Michelle and Paul as they went to work in central Brisbane and, in the evenings, catch a taxi home at about eight o'clock.

Dinner was a lovely meal, always. There were plenty of cooked choices, all very tasty. It was quite a task to choose which to have, but we would share a little each and spend the time between dinner and Marise's departure watching TV and talking. We talked a lot about the farm and what would need to be done on our return. It all seemed so daunting to me, and I dare say scary to Marise, but we were determined to battle our way through.

Marise would head off about eight o'clock, and I would read and watch a little tele and chat to the nurses. There was a wonderful Scottish nurse who was so very nice. She would sit and talk to me about anything. Quite often, I would break down and cry. She would reassure me and brighten my spirits. I was so grateful for her time. Her name was Louise, though I cannot remember her surname for the life of me. Louise had a beautiful Scottish accent, unsurprisingly sweet, soft, and warm. It is never a wonder to me that some people are just meant to be nurses. Their compassion, empathy, and kindness endear them to their patients. Well, to me, anyway.

Another of the nurses was a delightful young woman who wore the most colourful earrings, hairbands, and lipstick. We managed to work our way through a monster bag of lolly snakes over the period of a couple of days. I would sneak her a handful of snakes, which she would conceal on her person. The whole operation was quite clandestine, but only because we chose to make it so. There was obviously no hard rule about nurses sharing patients' lollies. She was such fun and put a smile on my face every time I saw her.

★ ★ ★

There were many bumps in the highway of my hospital stay. Mostly, I kept my personal pain or discomfort from the nurses. I saw no need to bother them with my dramas and did not see the point in getting any of them into trouble when an incident occurred. I would ask for help if needed or otherwise just work my way through it.

One day was particularly traumatic for me. The bed I was in was what I imagined to be a state-of-the-art, fully adjustable model. The mattress was an air mattress, which made whistling sounds of different tones when I moved around. For the first few days, I couldn't wait to be able to move a little, to make music from the novel mattress. The mattress was also heated, which I didn't know until early one morning when I awoke to discover the mattress had gone flat, and I was laying supported only by a couple of steel bars across the bedframe. I was so cold, and in such pain, but it was no one's fault—just something that apparently happens now and then, and so the day began.

The bed mattress was replaced, and that should have been that. But after lunch, and still in a reasonable amount of pain due to the bed fiasco, I was placed into a wheelchair to have a shower. As I have said, I was determined to be as independent as possible, so I put my hand up and offered to shower myself. Now, in a wheelchair, with a broken right arm, fractured right femur, broken foot, and being basically incapacitated, I sat in the shower area, awaiting my refreshing shower. The nurse ran me through the shower routine and then, after pointing out to me the button I could push to call for help if needed, left me to my own devices, as I said I would be fine.

The Harry Houdini skills required to shower turned out to be beyond my abilities, but a general wash was achieved, and I was soon ready to be taken back to bed. I waited for quite a while and became cold, so I turned on the water again. I waited a while longer, in hope, before deciding to push the red button. Now, I did not want to annoy the nurses. They were obviously busy, and they would come for me eventually, but how long could I sit here in pain? Not much longer, I assure you. So, Dean, just give that little red button a push.

Well, for the life of me, I couldn't reach the button. Every attempt bought more pain and frustration. The next obvious plan of attack would involve me calling out for help. The drama now became my aversion to making a scene. I certainly didn't want to be seen as needy or want to be the centre of attention. Still, with few avenues remaining, calling for help it would be. My first few calls for assistance seemed barely audible to me, and they were apparently also inaudible to anyone outside the shower room.

The continuous effort of trying to get the attention of someone outside, and a slight panic, led to me becoming quite hot and weak. What seemed like hours passed. Finally, one of the nurses came to check why the door was closed. The dear nurse was full of apologies, and I was equally thankful for the extraction from my little prison. So, back to bed.

I was really in quite a state by this stage. I felt so vulnerable and alone. Marise wasn't about for some reason, and I was hurting. I then received a phone call from a dear friend, and through the tears, I managed to have a little chat before telling her that I couldn't talk any more. I curled myself into the foetal position—a position I had not been familiar with till that day. I pulled the sheets over my head and just cried. I felt completely drained, shattered, and hopeless.

These were feelings I would have to learn to work my way through many times over the next few years. That day was right up there with the toughest I'd had. Boy oh boy; there were plenty more of those days to come.

★ ★ ★

My right forearm had been in a back slab and was causing me little drama. At this stage, I did have some movement in the arm, which meant I could move it about a little to get comfortable, the pursuit of which proved to be a full-time occupation. The next … well, let's say, the *only* battle I fought with the nurses and doctors was in regard to my arm.

As I have said, I really only had the use of my left arm, though the little movement in my right was very important to me for independence and comfort's sake. Enter one older, determined nurse to challenge, my stubborn—though still, I believed, reasonable—side. The battle lines would be drawn around my poor right forearm. Who would take up the fight on its behalf? Well, me, who else?

So this nurse enters after breakfast and asks me what colour plaster I would like on my arm. This seemed quite a reasonable enquiry. My arm would need to be in plaster for stability when I left hospital—something I was aware of. So her request seemed to offer up little concern to me. How wrong could I be?

The situation took an unexpected turn when she inferred that my arm would have to be in a full plaster, to well above my elbow. Now, my forearm was plated, and I saw no need for a full plaster. The plate would give sufficient support to the break with a half-arm plaster. Why the overkill? I asked. The nurse's response was that it just had to be, I had no choice, and my professional opinion carried little weight. So after breakfast, I was plastered up in a maroon plaster—there was no blue, oh, the indignity of it all!—to well above my elbow. My indignation was barely obvious; I chose a silent protest at this stage.

However, the next morning, when the doctors did their rounds, I was ready. I enquired of the doctor if he deemed it necessary for my arm to be in a full plaster. He was unsure but assured me that he would bring the matter up at the daily meeting held by the team responsible for my care. I was happy with that.

The next morning, I asked him if the matter had been resolved, and he was happy to inform me that a half-arm plaster would be sufficient. He would inform the nurses of the change. So, later that morning, the same nurse, obviously quite indignant over the turn of events, oversaw the removal of the full plaster and the application of a nice blue half plaster. Apparently, they found some blue colouring. Maybe they had to import some from south of the border, down Mexico way.

A little win meant so much to me. There was little I was in control of. I hope I wasn't being unreasonable, and I certainly didn't want to cause any problems, but I truly needed that little bit of movement in that arm. It was so much more comfortable. Oh, how I needed that!

★ ★ ★

There would obviously come a time when the talk about insurance would arise, as we all knew it must. At the time, it seemed of little consequence. I would be fully recovered in three or four months, at the most, and tossing the whole accident thing aside. But the wheels of litigation must be lubricated, and it was our turn to do the greasing.

Paul was friends with a lawyer, and he had arranged for this man to meet with us, in hospital, to discuss the ins and outs of the business. He arrived one morning while we were all present and very nicely set about making us aware of our possible entitlements under Queensland third-party law. Russell was a lovely bloke and made us feel at ease. I am sure it is all a part of their training, but even so, he was very pleasant and courteous. By the end of the meeting, we had signed the paperwork to enlist him as our legal representative in the matter. It was all foreign to us, and we wondered if we had just rushed into something.

The meeting with Russell was the beginning of an unbelievably long, protracted, twisty-turny legal journey that would bubble along beside us and over us for years to come. The dynamics of our journey with the lawyers and the RACQ were, and still are, mysteries to me. We did have the choice of representing ourselves in the matter. Thank God we did not choose to. We would have ended up financially devastated, at the least.

I have maintained, from the beginning, that I could deal with doctors and specialists day after day if necessary, but I never looked forward to dealing with lawyers or insurance companies. Maybe we have a deep-seated suspicion of their motives and a fear of their ability to charge exorbitant amounts of money for nothing in particular. The institution, as a whole, is untrusted by the general public, and few of our collective experiences managed to improve the perception. I had hoped that our experience would be the exception to the rule.

★ ★ ★

By day five or six, I was strong enough to go for a little trip in my wheelchair. Marise took me down to the hospital cafe for a little treat. It was a wondrous occasion—to be clear of those four walls, if only for half an hour or so. I felt invigorated by the contact with other people besides the nurses and doctors. I felt part of the world again. Just to sit amongst people going about their normal day-to-day lives, ordering coffee, kids running about, even looking outside and seeing trees and plants, lifted my spirits. I am sure I smiled. I hope I smiled, even if only to let Marise know that somewhere inside, I was still there, still me.

This wasn't the only time I had left the ward. There had been multiple visits to X-ray, and quite uncomfortable excursions they tended to be—not as pleasant as the cafe trip. I would be transferred to another bed, to be wheeled to the X-ray department, then transferred again onto the X-ray table. Many orderlies would do their best to make the transfers as painless as possible, but sadly, no amount of care could prevent the pain that would inevitably result from the many movements.

Prior to any of these movements, I would be offered Endone tablets, or Panadol, to give me a little buffer from the expected pain. On my return, more painkillers would be offered, and most times accepted gladly. Still, the adoption of the foetal position and some quiet time on my return to the ward was necessary to recover. I found little joy in the X-ray adventures. Still, they were a necessity, and were on the whole accomplished with the utmost care.

★ ★ ★

My partner in crime Steve's condition fluctuated. His injuries were so extensive, they impacted upon him greatly. Every time he had to be rolled, the pain he would go through was frightful. He was not keen on movement and would have dearly loved to be able to lie in one position without the torture of rolling. But to reduce the risk of pressure sores, the rolling was necessary.

The process would involve two orderlies and a nurse, Steve holding his breath to help with the pain, and a great deal of pushing, pulling, and sliding, accentuated by Steve's cries of pain. After the ordeal, he lay in pain once again until his body finally settled to the new position—until the whole process of pain building up began again.

One morning, Steve didn't seem himself. He was quiet, not keen to converse, and in a mountain of pain. Over the next twenty-four hours, he slipped further, and I held grave concerns for him. His breathing was laboured, and a constant stream of doctors and nurses coming to his bedside made it obvious that something was wrong. After X-rays and many tests, it was discovered that Steve was having respiratory problems, and he would have to have a tube inserted into his lung to drain fluid off it.

Steve's condition must have been quite serious, as it was decided that the procedure would have to be performed in the ward. For the next hour or so, a hive of activity swarmed around his bed, as he lay there in a drugged state to alleviate his pain. About midday, preparations were complete, and the doctor and nurses were in attendance for the procedure.

What followed was truly frightful. The pain my dear friend went through as the doctor attempted to make an incision through his chest wall to facilitate the insertion of a drain was awful. Steve lay there conscious throughout, crying and begging for the doctor to stop, until he could object no more due to the pain. The thought of Steve's pleading chills me still.

The doctor continued for what seemed like an hour (though in fact it may have been only twenty minutes, I am not sure) while giving a running commentary to all in the ward. This sounds macabre, but I do not mean to imply that he was describing every cut or twist of the procedure. He merely vocalised his frustration at his inability to perform the procedure, saying repeatedly that he thought he could just get it with another attempt. This went on and on, accompanied by Steve's ever failing cries for the whole thing to stop and his moans of excruciating pain, which were becoming weaker from exhaustion.

The nightmare had cleared the ward of all who could leave. The patients capable of walking and the nursing staff not involved in the procedure all vacated to the relative peace outside the ward. Apart from those attending Steve, thankfully from behind drawn curtains, I was the only other soul in the ward. I would have done anything to extricate myself also, but I had not the means to do so.

Eventually, the doctor admitted defeat, much to his disgust. I sensed that he somehow blamed Steve for not having the strength to see the thing through. He withdrew from the battlefield and left my dear friend battered, beaten, and worn to a frazzle, lying in a pool of sweat and a world of pain. Steve was shattered, and I imagine—well, I hope—that he was sedated heavily. He was barely with us for the next few hours. He lay in rest while everyone made a staggered return to the ward.

The ordeal was over. Steve recovered from the procedure and the fluid on his lung, by some other medical means I imagine, and we returned to the normality of our little world. I had been given a lesson in the cruel kindness sometimes associated with medicine. In the process of treating some medical conditions, the pain of the treatment can be far more brutal than the condition itself.

Maybe sometimes an alternative treatment could have achieved the same result with less pain and stress. In Steve's case, he did recover from the lung condition without the drain being inserted. Maybe he was just fortunate, but the pain he went through that day—well, I hope I never have to endure similar.

The next day, Steve was back with us, thank God, and as his strength returned, so did his sense of humour. We continued on, putting the day before to the back of our minds. Well, maybe to the back, but still so vivid!

3. STANLEY

Stanley … well, I can only hope that I was able to leave a lasting memory for Stanley, as he certainly left me with many wonderful memories, all associated with my hospital stay in Brisbane. I doubt if many people would admit to making happy memories in hospital, but I did!

It was likely two or three days into my stay when I made Stanley's acquaintance. He was obviously in his early twenties, slight, quiet, so very polite, so generous and kind. Stanley was a young nursing exchange student from, as best as I can remember, Malaysia. I apologise to Stanley if perchance you read this one day and I have not managed to acknowledge your proper country of origin.

Stanley was introduced to me, and all the other patients, early one morning as a trainee. The nurse on duty very politely asked us if we would allow Stanley to observe as the nurses provided care to us over the next few days. Furthermore, would we allow Stanley to assist and in fact carry out some or our routine observations, simple procedures, and care?

Much to my surprise, though understandably, the other patients declined the invitation to allow Stanley this wonderful opportunity to gain some valuable hands-on experience at this wonderful facility. I, on the other hand, nearly jumped out of bed to embrace Stanley, welcome him heartily, and put my body at his disposal. That may be a slight exaggeration, but I was delighted to meet Stanley, and I did offer my body as a canvas for his training. It was an offer Stanley seemed more than happy to accept, and the seeds of a fruitful relationship were sown then and there.

For the shifts when Stanley was on the floor, I was his guinea pig. He bathed me, took my temperature, helped move me, and gave me my blood-thinning injections. On one night when I was painfully constipated, Stanley was given the privilege of administering me with a suppository. Well, *privilege* may be a slight misrepresentation of the situation, but for my part, it may as well have been Stanley as any other nurse who assisted me that evening. I felt honoured to have been able to give him that opportunity.

Every time Stanley came into the ward, we exchanged hearty smiles. He was obviously delighted that I allowed him to use me as a training tool. One morning, a nurse informed me that I was the only patient on the floor who Stanley was doing his exchange training on. None of the others would allow Stanley to touch them.

Over the entire period of my hospitalisation and convalescence, I was confronted with the realisation that many people were far from accepting, not only on ethnic grounds but sadly on gender grounds as well. It saddened me. I had, in fact, grown up in a suspicious environment. Many people I was close to, and many more I knew well, were quite homophobic and openly racist, but I'd held out a hope that in the big brave world outside my little bubble, these suspicions were less prevalent. But alas, not so.

★ ★ ★

Now, I have to be honest at this point. I was amongst those who looked with suspicion at people of different ethnic backgrounds. Zoe, our youngest child, had a congenital heart disorder from birth, and we were to spend many days attending specialists in Sydney until she was about sixteen. We travelled around Sydney, predominately by train, and the ethnic diversity of Sydney was a far cry from the ethnic monoculture of our own backyard.

Though over time I grew more comfortable with the ethnic diversity, I was never totally at ease with it, and sometimes I felt quite ill at ease, particularly if we were travelling by train at night. I was even then challenged by my behaviour. I knew my suspicions had little foundation, but the means or the catalyst to change had not presented itself till the accident. It became a defining moment for me, a light-switch moment, one that opened my heart and mind to the all-embracing tolerance and acceptance that brightened my world more and more as time passed.

★ ★ ★

After about ten days, the nurse on duty asked me if I would allow Stanley to take out my hundred or so staples. No trouble, Stanley—go for your life. At first, I think he was very cautious, as I fear I would have been in the same situation. I assured Stanley he was causing me no discomfort, and he completed the task with much delight. He was so very proud of himself, and he thanked me more than once for allowing him to remove them.

I do hope Stanley found his calling in life. If it came to be that nursing was his chosen career, I would be delighted if our meeting and shared experiences helped him along his path.

4. GET ME OUT OF HERE!

From about day six, I had my mind set on getting out of the place. I was feeling sharper, the morphine and associated drugs effects were starting to wear off, and my mind was on home. I was probably being a real arsehole. I wanted my life back, no matter the cost or situation. I was now beginning to take in the impact the accident was having on every one of us, and I had begun to feel responsible for all their woes.

My dear Sarah had had a horrible time of it in Redcliffe Hospital, where she was taken after the crash. She had not been allowed to eat for three days, as they were preparing to operate on her forearm every day, but the ops had been postponed every day. The dear girl was separated from her family, was very emotional, and had been chastised severely by one nurse for being a sook. Michelle and Paul were visiting her daily, with Marise and the girls, but Sarah's predicament was painful and lonely—and she was so worried about me.

I knew little of her situation till months later. Rightly or wrongly, I was spared the details. Even so, I felt her predicament was solely my fault, and to this day, some things just aren't easy to get over.

Dad, Mum, Hannah, and Zoe had returned home. They were to attend our cousin's twenty-first and, rightly so, needed to be home. Zoe was halfway through her HSC year. She'd missed her trial exams and had to organise to take them later. Hannah was at uni. Both of them had to try to study and get back into a normal routine.

Dad was under immense pressure. I am sure he worked far too hard over the next few years. It surely took its toll on his health, which was already greatly compromised. Marise had the weight of the world on her shoulders, dear girl, and she too needed not the pressure and drama that beset her at this stage and continued for a couple of years. Meanwhile, I selfishly tore ahead with my plans for an escape. Well, not exactly, but I was determined to get home.

Unable to rectify the dramas and worries of all concerned from the confines of my little world, I took in hand the few things I could manage: my recovery and getting home. I began to do stretches and whatever exercises I could manage from my bed, given the restrictions imposed upon me by my ailments. Whenever I woke in the night, I would do sit-ups, arm curls, and fist pumps, as many as I could manage. I would wake a few hours later and do the same.

I began to feel more energised and enthused. I surely needed to feel better, working towards my goal. I thought that on my return home, I could take on the challenge of dealing with all the damage I felt responsible for. But get home I must!

★ ★ ★

Opportunities to facilitate my repatriation began to present themselves. There was at first a plan to have me transferred to the border by ambulance, then transferred to an ambulance from

New South Wales, and then on to Tamworth Hospital for a couple of days before my release to go home. The logistics of this exercise were obviously beyond the scope or abilities of both state health systems. Thank God for that—there was no way I could have managed six or seven hours bouncing around in an ambulance.

Every morning, I would ask how preparations were coming along, and the answer daily was little different. It became apparent to me that my situation was causing much angst in health-department circles. There seemed to be many obstacles and complications in my repatriation, and I was being a very squeaky wheel, one who refused to be quietened by a squirt of oil.

As the days went by, my frustrations were compounding. I was feeling very guilty that Marise was suffering away from home and support—though Michelle and Paul were unbelievable in their love care and help. I will be forever in their debt. Marise was adamant that things were OK. Still, I was undaunted in my efforts to return home.

So the days went by. Physio was giving me the skills and upper body strength to make bed-to-wheelchair transfers and vice versa, which would give me some independence and lighten the burden on my carers. I was sure that I could tick all of the boxes required so that my care level would be minimal. This delusional train of thought would evidently have the expected ramifications. I would be a drain and a headache for all around me in the course of my recovery. I just couldn't see it then.

★ ★ ★

Steve also had an altercation with the nurse who had insisted on me wearing a gown and my bed being made to hospital guidelines. His wife, Jillian, needed to return to Toowoomba so that the girls could get back to school, and so they would only be able to visit once a week. Steve was very upset about the situation, and it was very tough on Jillian to leave Steve for these extended periods of time. But they could see few other options.

The nurse came in to have a chat with Steve, and once more, I was feeling for him. The nurse tore into him, suggesting that he was unreasonably selfish and that he had to consider Jillian's and the girls' needs and situation. She was quite scathing in her questioning of him.

Steve was by now quite upset himself, and I felt like tearing into the nurse in his defence. But to my surprise, she changed her tack there and then and was very compassionate and understanding. She reassured Steve that all the nursing staff were there for him and that all would be well. The dear nurse's blunt appraisal of the situation, and then understanding and compassion, had helped Steve realise what needed to be done and how, with everyone working together, he would be cared for and comforted through Jillian's absence.

I had to take my hat off to the nurse. Obviously, with many years of experience, she had learned a trick or two, and she knew what was required in the situation. All would be well, she knew, and now also did Steve. Jillian was obviously relieved by Steve's more reasonable outlook.

★ ★ ★

The sun came up every morning, and every day my strength returned a little, as did my resolve to be home, until one morning, to my surprise, I was informed that I would be transferred that day to the Armidale Hospital by air transfer. I was delighted. When Marise arrived at the hospital that morning, there was much to be organised before we could both get home to New South Wales.

It was too late for Michelle to organise an air flight home for Marise that day, but she was able to get Marise on a flight to Tamworth early the next morning. There were a few things to be sent home that were too big for the trip with me, so Marise would have to get them back to Michelle's and Paul's to take on the plane with her. We waited patiently as nurses and doctors came and went with papers to sign and tests to be carried out. The process dragged on and on, and as the hours swept by, it seemed unlikely that I would be out of there that day.

Surprisingly, however, by about two in the afternoon, all preparations had been made, all boxes had been ticked, and word came through that the ambulance that would take me to the airfield had arrived. I was transferred onto another bed to be taken down to emergency. When I arrived at emergency, I was then transferred to a gurney. It became immediately obvious to me that the trip would be one best described as painful, but in fact, it was torture.

Just above my hips on the gurney was a metal support bar that was immediately uncomfortable, but I thought there would be no drama; I would only be on the gurney till we arrived at the airfield. I have quite often made the mistake of seeing the best-case scenario in an awkward situation, and this proved to be one of those times. The transfer to the Archibald Airfield was short and sweet—still painful, bloody bar—but the gods of fair play must have taken the afternoon off and the gods of shit things were filling in.

On arrival at the airfield, we were greeted by closed gates. Now, that was not much of a surprise; we can't just have anyone driving in and out of an airfield, can we? Let's just get on the radio, call in, and see what's going on. A little radio tag, just a few enquiries as to whether someone may be able to open the gates for us. "Yes, well, we are waiting for an air transfer plane to take a patient to Armidale. We need to get into the airfield. ... What do you mean, you don't know anything about this transfer? ... Well, how long will it take to find someone to come and open the gates? ... OK, we will just wait."

The time crawled by. The bar had by now pressed my spine through to my ribs. I may not have mentioned that I was strapped onto this instrument of torture and was unable to move. I could not roll from side to side or shuffle up or down. The person responsible for the design and manufacture of this device should be very reassured that most other human experiences are far less painful than an outing on one of their gurneys.

On reflection, maybe they had forgotten to put a mattress on the gurney before I was attached to it. Not likely, but I cannot for the life of me imagine how the flaw in its design had not been brought to someone's attention before this. Another possibility is that everyone who has ever experienced the joy of a trip on one of these hideous contraptions has been so relieved on their extraction that they have failed to inform anyone of their painful experience—or have, due to the pain they were in, been rendered incapable of speech.

In time, a young man arrived and opened the gates. We were in. Surely the gods of fortune were back on the job. Ha ha!

Within another thirty minutes or so the plane landed—a small plane, a toyish-looking plane. It was a private plane from Coffs Harbour that did patient transfers. They had provided the cheapest quote for the job, apparently. A door opened and a pilot and nurse emerged. At least I would have company; not that I thought that I would have to fly the thing by myself, but I did expect a little bigger plane.

I was removed from the ambulance and inserted into the plane—on the same gurney! Oh no! Could this be true? Afraid so. Bloody bar! Strapped into the plane now, no movement possible still, in fact possibly less. This would be another memorable trip. I could feel it in my bones, in particular my spine.

As the pilot prepared for take-off, the nurse went through the initiation—in case of an emergency, the exits are here, pointing to the door and an exit sign. Thank you very much. Strapped snuggly, though painfully, into the plane, there seemed little chance of a man with a broken leg, arm, and foot being in need of said exits. If this plane goes down, I wish the pilot and nurse all the best in their safe escape. If you don't mind. I'll just go down with the plane.

We were soon in the air, and me being a rather virginal flyer—or, more to point, airborne passenger—well, stress levels were high. The nurse was very nice and offered a multitude of assurances. I obviously looked in need of them. What I do remember needing was some relief from the pain still radiating from my lower back. I mentioned this to her, at an appropriate time, about one minute into the flight, and she produced the obligatory Panadols. Ah, the hope of relief. Washing them down with a sip of water, I wished them well on their journey to my nervous system, and ultimately, to the base of my spine.

Within no time at all, we were screaming towards Armidale, and glory be, a rather daunting night-time thunderstorm as well. The lightning was spectacular and would have been a real spectacle from the relative safety of the ground, but it took on an ominous complexion from my vantage point, and visions of light planes being buffeted by storms and struck by lightning played out in my mind as we careered onward.

Now whether we flew around the storm or not, I will never know. My recollection, though, is that we tore straight into its fury, with the pilot laughing madly like a pirate sailing his ship into a maelstrom. No, that was not the case; he wasn't laughing madly. But I do think we flew very close by. It certainly felt that way, as we were buffeted around and lightning flashed ever so close.

We drew ever closer to Armidale, and the last fifteen minutes or so of our flight was rather uneventful, which I was grateful for. Salvation from this infernal gurney seemed at hand. The nurse went through the checklist before landing, checked all belts, and strapped herself in. We were soon on the ground and coasting to a stop.

One more small fact about the flight: there seemed to be little heating in the plane. Now I don't know for sure if indeed they did have heating, but I was frozen on arrival at Armidale, and when I was at last removed from the plane, the bitter wind that greeted me was a welcome home of sorts. Though very cold and numb beneath my hips, I was inching closer towards where I wanted to be: home.

★ ★ ★

An ambulance was waiting for me, and at last I was extricated from the torture of the gurney and placed on the relative luxury of another without an offending bar. The ambulance had been sourced from Gunnedah, 160 kilometres away; none were available in Armidale or Tamworth, so Gunnedah was the next closest. The expense for the whole exercise was obviously massive, and I was feeling a little precious in regard to my behaviour, but I knew that if I had stayed in Brisbane until I was able to return home by any other means, I would have been there for a couple of months, and that was not possible. Marise was determined to be by my side, and the farm needed immediate attention. Marise needed to be home, and so I had to be as near as possible. Armidale was it.

I was safely placed into the ambulance, and we were soon on our way for the four-kilometre trip to the Armidale hospital. Such comfort and warmth in the ambulance! My fortunes had turned, and all was well. Ah, famous last words! I was still feeling it, as in the Toyota adds, as I was wheeled into the hospital and placed onto another bed. The paramedics said their farewells, and I settled into my new surrounds.

I knew a couple of the staff, so we had a little chat. Things were rather quiet. It was about ten in the evening, I imagine, and to my surprise, it soon became apparent that I was an unexpected guest. I have no doubt at all that at a certain level in the chain of command, someone knew I was arriving, but obviously the message had not had time to filter down to the staff on duty. So there was an hour or so to be spent in a corridor, waiting for a bed.

Because the wheels set in motion for my extradition from Brisbane had been turning all day, I had dropped off the meal list at the Princess Alexandra after breakfast. I had managed a cuppa and biscuit for morning tea but hadn't eaten since, so I was a tad hungry. I mentioned this in passing to the nurses at Armidale, and they managed to find some sandwiches, which I gratefully accepted, and then a nice cup of tea, and all was well. At last, a bed was found for me in the surgical ward, and I was wheeled off to my new abode through the maze of corridors and rooms we went in till I was tucked in for the night.

That night would be a good candidate for the worst night I have ever put in. The bed was so hard and cold, I froze and ached. There was no position I could get in that would give me relief. There was no handhold hanging from above to lift myself, and the night dragged on and on. I did call a nurse and ask for another blanket, but it did little to warm me. I had sweltered in Brisbane, and now I froze in Armidale. I was gutted.

By morning, I was a wreck. I was shattered. There was no way I could do this. I knew recovery would be tough, but I needed to be at least comfortable to get by, and there was little comfort to be had here. That is not to say that the nurses were not kind or caring, but given the facilities they had to work with, they could do little more. So it seemed to me that I would somehow have to just suck it up. I doubted my ability to suck hard enough.

Breakfast was a rather Spartan affair. I can't remember for sure what it comprised of, but it didn't elicit any long-term or short-term wow. Given my state of mind at the time, possibly nothing would have. I had pinned so much on my return to Armidale; I had fought and craved it for two weeks. And now it was a misery—a painful gaol, not a pleasant resort.

So maybe much of the fault fell on me. The spiralling-out-of-control feeling I let take over now washed me out to sea, far from any comfort or joy I could imagine. I was in a dark place. What to do, what to do?

★ ★ ★

After a nice breakfast, I was assisted to the shower by a lovely male nurse. The warm water rushing over my cold aching body was a godsend. I felt a little more comfortable. I could have sat there all day, but all too soon, I was dried, dressed, and on my way back to the room. The nurse helped me into a hard vinyl-covered chair beside a window that let through a faint winter's light but no warmth. I sat wrapped in blankets, shivering.

By morning tea, I had warmed a little. A cuppa and biscuits helped. But I needed more—more food, more something to take my mind off my woes. Ah, TV?

I asked the male nurse who brought my cuppa what the process was for getting a TV. He told me that one would have to be rented from downtown, and it probably wouldn't be able to be set up for a day or so. Another blow. In the midst of this conversation, where I must have been losing hope, I mentioned that I had private health cover and maybe it could hurry things along.

"Well, what in the hell are you doing here then?" he exclaimed. "You should move to the private hospital next door. It's a bloody sight better than this place."

My ears pricked. That sounded promising. "How do I go about getting in there?" I asked. He said he would go and find someone who could help me and was off. I tried not to get my hopes up; knowing my luck of late, there would be no beds available in the private hospital. I would have to battle on here. *Please God, let there be a bed.*

★ ★ ★

Within a few hours, all was arranged, and I was once more wheeled to another room—a private room, a beautiful room. There was a fully adjustable bed, large reclining lounge chair, an en suite, and a big window with a lovely garden view. I took in a deep breath and knew that this would work. If I was going to recover quickly, this was the place to do so.

I was helped into the lounge chair. It was so comfortable. Someone brought me a cuppa and cream biscuits. Yes, cream biscuits! I didn't know they allowed them in hospitals. Old faithfuls were the only fare I thought they were allowed to serve. (A bloke I used to shear for always referred to the plain Arnott's biscuits as *old faithfuls*. They were the only biscuits his wife would give him, and maybe she had been a nurse? He did have seven teaspoons of sugar in his tea, though, so maybe she thought he had enough sugar in his diet already!)

The surprises didn't end there. It was a continuous parade of cakes and slices, for that matter. A cuppa and a snack could be had at any time. Most nights, or in the early mornings, I was offered a bowl of fresh fruit salad, which I could not resist. I was putting on weight, but I knew I needed to eat to recover, so off we go.

If you desired, you could also have a bottle of beer or a glass of wine with your dinner, but I never did. I didn't feel like a drink. It would be a month or so till I had a beer, and by then, it was a real treat.

★ ★ ★

I had a constant stream of visitors—some a little more hard work than others, but still, I enjoyed the company. My routine was quite disciplined. I was awakened by blood pressure checks, cups of tea, and medication. I would watch some morning TV and then read most of the day—newspapers and books—of course interrupted by more blood pressure checks. But the days filled in, and boredom was generally allayed.

I was now more fiercely determined to be independent, and looking back, I now see the danger this posed to me and the staff. I began to get out of bed by myself, and I could even manage to hop and shuffle to the toilet or shower and take care of all those needs myself. The amount of energy expended in these ventures was unbelievable, and after each such excursion, a great deal of time was needed to recover. But I kept telling myself that I was building my strength up again, which I was, though ever so slowly.

I couldn't believe how weak I was or had become. Even a short period of inactivity results in muscle loss, and that is where I was now. I still did all the stretches and exercises I could manage, but if there was any great improvement at this stage, it was far from evident. I do think it was all beneficial though. I was feeling far less pain and discomfort, which was a relief, and with a little more mobility. I was feeling better about myself.

Marise came to visit me every couple of days. It was wonderful to see her, but I struggled to cope with the dilemma surrounding her having to be at home doing all of the work. Now, Marise wasn't alone on the farm. Dad was there every day, helping as he could and offering company to Marise. But he was not well enough to be doing very much, and that tore at me also. I could be of no practical help, and most probably I was more of a worry and concern for her, one which she could well do without, given the circumstances.

In all honesty, I was probably feeling very sorry for myself, very useless, very uncertain about the future, and more than anything else, concerned about the person I would be when I recovered. I still grappled with the prospect of never being able to shear again, never being able to contribute to the family finances, even being able to help around the farm. I was far from depression at this stage as I blindly pushed towards recovery and, even more importantly, getting home.

There were various outings, mostly trips to the X-ray department. These were logistical productions in their own right, with transfers and the like, but they were much less painful as the days went by, and a change of scenery was always appreciated. After these adventures, it was always nice to return to my room, the comfort of that lounge, the security it offered. When we lose control of our circumstances and our environment, we search for a place of security and serenity where we can shelter from the things we can't control, and that room was my cave, where I could be in some control.

Oh! How I longed to be home. I continuously enquired about what boxes I would have to tick to be able to go home. I could transfer from bed to chair, I could hop, but that wasn't allowed, as it would put too much shock on my thigh. I could brush my hair and teeth. What more was needed? Well, apparently, I needed to be able to walk with the aid of a walker, up and down the hall at the hospital, safely and confidently. I worked on that daily. If this was the one thing that would procure my release, then so be it: walk, walk, walk.

One day when Marise came for a visit, she was so run-down, I could see it in her eyes and sense it in her conversation. I was so concerned for her, but there was little I could do. As she was leaving, I asked her to ring me when she arrived home, just to let me know she was safe and sound. It was dark when she left, which heightened my anxiety further. I was shattered to see her leave and so wished I could go with her.

Marise left at about six o'clock, and I expected a call from her about seven thirty. I watched the clock, barely taking my eyes off it. By eight o'clock, I was concerned. By eight thirty, I was having a heart attack. I really believed I was. I have never been so scared in my life. I lay there in bed, sweating, shaking, my heart pounding in my chest, in my throat even. I did not want to die here, like this.

I called for the nurse. She immediately gave me an ECG, which showed that I was not having a heart attack but a panic attack. I was greatly relieved, but it took half an hour or so of her kindness and understanding to talk me down. Only after I rang and talked to Marise did I finally manage to settle. Marise had stopped off somewhere for dinner and was too tired on returning home to give me a call straight away, which was entirely understandable given the circumstances. That was the worst evening I have ever gone through. Even the accident didn't affect me like that panic attack had. I hope never to have another one.

★ ★ ★

It was delightful to see friends and relatives, though my strength was always tested by the visits and after, I needed a good rest. One such visit was from dear friends of ours, Dave and Sonya. Sonya was a very experienced nurse and was, as ever, straight down the line and pulling no punches. From her experience, she was so kind to let me know that after a severe hip trauma, it was quite often the case that the patient would, within ten or so years, require a hip replacement. Given the situation I was in at the time, and the concerns and fears I held, the last thing I needed was this information. It gutted me.

Why, I was only fifty. What the hell would life be like the next few years if this was to be the case? I must confess: the next thirty minutes of their visit was rather painful and offered little in the way of reassurance or hope. I was in a very glum frame of mind for the rest of the day, and it has, even after six years, been a constant worry to me.

A hip replacement would mean a real change in my lifestyle, one I was not at all pleased about. Talking to people I know who have had replacements, I learned that a replacement hip's lifespan is about fifteen years, and that is if your lifestyle does not place too much strain or weight on the joint. I would struggle to do the required farm work, as it is very heavy and repetitive.

★ ★ ★

I struck up a friendship with one of the wards-men, who was forever offering me treats, biscuits, cakes, fruit platters, and anything that was available. He brought newspapers early in the mornings with my cuppa and always stayed a while and chatted. He was so pleasant and made the days a pleasure, though as was still the case, the nights were a solitary, lonely time. I managed them only with the help of sleeping tablets.

I pondered whether I would ever sleep soundly again. I had never slept well, always waking to the slightest noise, but now sleep took on another dimension. It was not easy to get enough sleep. I would steal an hour or so during the day. This would keep me rested and sane.

The staff at the hospital was remarkable, as had been the staff at the Princess Alexandra. As hard as I tried to be as little a burden on their time or resources as possible, I still felt guilty about the assistance I required, and this also worried me in regard to my return home. My selfishness seemed to know no bounds. After four or so days, my next focus was, once again, on getting home. I did not want to be a drain on Marise's strength and time, but regardless, I pushed on towards my ultimate goal: liberation and repatriation. Full steam ahead was my modus operandi.

I cannot sing Marise's praises enough. Her ability to deal with all that was going on in our world—which had been turned upside down and twisted and turned till it was barely recognisable as our world of a few weeks ago—was inspirational, to say the least. She had to deal with the farm that was in a state of drought by now; Dad, who was beside himself with worry; and Zoe, who was trying to keep on track with her studies; and her biggest headache, me!

I can only imagine her other concerns were far easier to manage than I, and I wish that had not been the case. I do not consider myself a selfish person, but the person I had become was, in many respects, just that. I did not demand but played on people's sympathy and compassion to get my way. I know I would sulk a little, cry now and then, pull on Marise's heartstrings, and hopefully get my way. I am not proud at all of my behaviour, though at the time, in my mind, it was quite justifiable. I wanted my previous life back; that was all, no more, no less. In that respect, the prospects were dim.

One of the criteria I had to meet to facilitate my release was mobility. I had to be able to use a walker to get around—no great distances, but enough to get to the toilet, for example. I practiced two or three times a day, inching my way up and down the corridor. The exercise was draining and sapped me completely. I was a real wreck. My God, would this be my life? I couldn't imagine the future like this.

At last, the day came when my relentless pushing finally resulted in my release. On reflection, I know I was not ready to return home. I knew it then, deep inside, but it was conveniently hidden from view. Given how protracted my recovery was to be, I doubt if another week in hospital would have made any difference.

★ ★ ★

Marise was set to come and pick me up midmorning, and I would be free—well, as free as a man who cannot walk can possibly be. With the paperwork done, and all my bits and pieces packed, I was wheeled out into the revelation of a New England winter's day. Shit, it was cold. In the three or so weeks since the accident, winter had arrived, and my habitat had been one of constant warmth and comfort, apart from the night in the Armidale hospital. The blast of the winter's air upon my face sent shivers through me and woke me from my delusional state. The reality of what was to come these next few months met me at the front door of the hospital.

I once more thanked the dear staff who had put up with me the past week. Then I shuffled and strained into the car and was chauffeured away by my dear wife, who must have had mixed feelings about the whole thing by now.

The first stop was the chemist, where the required painkillers and such were acquired. Marise did a quick grocery shop while I sat in the luxury of our ute, as happy as a pig in shit. The drive home was wonderful—to be outside in familiar surroundings was so stimulating, I felt as if a part of me that had been missing those past weeks had returned. The accident had made me appreciate the little things I had always taken for granted and given me a new perspective on life. That day, I drank it all up. I took in all the beauty and saw the beauty in the familiarity previously unrecognised, maybe deep down inside.

I promised myself that day that I would never be that unseeing being again. I would see, feel, and live every moment. I would take the time to look and wonder at everything. Daily, I now recall the moment in the car when we were being cut out by the wonderful rescue team, when I came to and saw the scene in front of me spin like an old movie till it stopped still. I saw those trees in front of me, so green, bright, vivid, rich, and glorious, and now I wanted and promised myself to look for that in all around me, and all I did, from that day forward.

That drive home was one such moment. Old was new, dull was bright, every corner offered up a new wonder, and as we neared home, the rush I felt was overwhelming. I knew I had been given a second chance. I realised a long tough road lay ahead. I wanted it all back, my life as before, but slowly I was realising that I would never be the same person. And I didn't want to be that person either. I could be a better person, much better in fact. I was unsure how or when or even what would be better, but a spark had been struck. A light of a promise of something took hold, and as dim as it now seemed, I would give myself to it, trust in it, and pray for it, my family, and myself.

We arrived home. I was so stiff and sore, I struggled to get out of the car but managed to do it slowly. Marise wheeled me inside to a house warmed by our now so greatly appreciated wood heater. I sat on the lounge for a while, had a lovely cup of tea, and made myself reacquainted with my dear wife and our world.

Sleep that night was once more only attainable by medication and was very uncomfortable, as sleep would be for many months to come. But in the comfort of my own bed, beside my darling Marise, I was so happy, so grateful, so very optimistic, and once again so delusional. What could possibly go wrong?

5. Home Again, Home Again, Jigerty Jig

The next day, Marise had organised some sheep shearing that needed to be done. Her brothers Garry and Graeme and three mates of ours—Warren Press, Darb Farrawell, and Nick Endicott—came to do the shearing. Graeme's wife, Robyn; my sister Debbie; and our niece Allie helped Marise do the wool and cooked us a lovely BBQ lunch. Dad and Mum came out also. Dad helped in the wool shed, and Mum babysat me.

I must admit, I have never felt as useless as I did that day. Those wonderful people were down in our shed, working to help us out, and I was laying on the lounge being babysat by my mum. They finished about four o'clock and all came up to the house for a quick catch-up and to see how I was. It was lovely to see them, all those mates. I felt so grateful for their efforts and humbled by their generosity. I could not imagine how I would ever be able to return the favour.

Oh, how I wished I could have been down there with them all day—in my environment, in my world. But there would be many more days like this one for me. I would have to get used to it somehow.

Marise was so capable, and I was so proud of her. I was seeing her through different eyes, and her drive to do all that needed doing was inspirational. It did, however, wear her down—caring for me, running the farm, doing all the housework. The toll that it was taking on her was difficult to deal with.

★ ★ ★

A typical day at this point in time played out like this: Marise would wake and get up about seven o'clock and start the wood heater. The weather was bitterly cold by now. She would get the house warmed up, prepare breakfast, and then get me out of bed. She would stand me in the walking frame and get me to the lounge room. We would have breakfast, then Marise would head out and start feeding up and doing the farm work. I would sit and read.

I was so into reading by this stage, I devoured books like there was no tomorrow. I would try not to turn the television on before three o'clock. I had decided to not fall into the trap of watching it all day, and reading helped get my mind back on track. My mind had become very slow, and even now, seven years later, I quite often suffer from long pauses in conversation, because simple words just won't come to me. At first, this was very disturbing, but I have learnt to live with it now. Even though it is still frustrating, I try to wait it out till the words come—probably much to the annoyance of those in conversation with me.

Marise would be out till midday, and even though she would tell me where she was going, I would continually worry about her. Riding a four-wheel bike around in hills can be dangerous at times. Fortunately, the worst that happened was she ran out of fuel a couple of times and had to walk a kilometre or so home to get more. On her return, she would make us some lunch and then head out again, quite often returning after dark.

After Marise had prepared dinner, we would sit down, and she would enjoy a little break before giving me a shower, preparing me for bed, washing up, having a shower herself, and then getting me into bed about nine o'clock. This went on day after day, and Marise's ability to keep this up was unbelievable. In my eyes, she was awesome, a saint, and I was hopelessly useless. This dragged on me daily and tore at my sense of worth. I wasn't much good for me and no good for Marise.

The girls' boyfriends—Matt, Jay, and Cameron—kept us in firewood. Our neighbours cut and delivered a load or two every so often as well. Once again, their generosity was overwhelming, and we were kept very comfortable as the winter crept on.

I had to use a bottle to urinate in, but I could manage to get to the toilet for other needs … say no more. The process was steady, but I could manage with caution.

The days rolled on, and I so wished to be out of the house. One nice day, Marise and Zoe helped me outside and sat me on the lawn. It was so enjoyable. I loved it, and as would continue to be the case, little outings and adventures brought such joy and wonder to me. I learnt to appreciate everything in a new light.

★ ★ ★

Six weeks after the accident, I made my first entries in our farm diary. They would be just updates on my condition for a while, but they would make for good reading later on and a handy reference for this story. Life was settling into a routine, but an uncomfortable one. The bane of my life, at this stage, was the plaster on my arm. It was becoming so annoying and uncomfortable.

I had often seen people scratching inside their plaster with a ruler or the like, in an attempt to alleviate the unbearable itch that accompanied plasters. I desperately wanted it gone. I pushed, pulled, tore at it—nothing gave any more than a minute's relief, and I whinged about it continuously. Marise was sympathetic but unrelenting in her opposition to me removing it. The girls toed the line and agreed with her.

Finally, after once more insisting that six weeks was sufficient healing for a broken arm in my professional opinion—ha ha!—I took a pair of heavy-duty scissors and removed the offending monster. Marise and the girls were unimpressed, insisting that it was not safe. Maybe the bones would not be healed, and I might reinjure them. "How?" I said. With a broken leg and foot, I could barely get about. It was not as if I would be going trail-bike riding.

I promised that I would be careful, very careful, and revelled in the ounce of freedom I had regained. Released from the discomfort of the plaster, I could manage from here on in. I told myself that, and it proved to be so.

There is something about trauma, and in particular recovering from trauma. I found that I had the strength to forge ahead, deal with the shit, and retain a bit of sanity on a daily basis … for about two weeks. I would then find myself unable to get out of bed. I would lay there most of the day, crying and feeling sorry for myself. The next day, I would be fine again. The only thing I could put this down to was that after two weeks or thereabouts of positive thought and the physical effort required in recovery, I would find myself physically and emotionally exhausted, and I needed that day of feeling sorry for myself before taking on that next two-week block. Though Marise didn't really understand the situation, she was very supportive of me on those days and tolerated my selfishness, or so it must have seemed to her.

★ ★ ★

The surgeon who had operated on me at the Princess Alexandria after the accident had wanted me to return to Brisbane for a six-week check-up. There was no way I could sit in a car for six or seven hours, and even flying up would have been problematic, so after some consultation, it was decided that I would see an orthopaedic surgeon in Armidale. Dr. Diebold had seen me while I was in the private hospital in Armidale, as I had to be transferred not only to the hospital but also to another doctor, and so Dr. Diebold was the one.

On May 17, I had my first trip back to town, saw the doctor, had X-rays, and visited a dear aunt of mine who was very unwell in hospital. It was very confronting to see her in such a low state, given the state I was in, but it was so wonderful to be able to say goodbye to her. The day out had been very long and tiring, and it took me a couple of days to recover, but we were off on the road to recovery.

Dr. Diebold had been happy with my healing and referred me to Rob Tindale, a physiotherapist in Armidale. I would see him in a week's time. The mood on the trip home was one of optimism. I felt relieved to be able to go to physio. I had never been before and was excited at the prospect.

★ ★ ★

A week later, I made the acquaintance of Rob Tindale. I was immediately taken in by his manner, interest in my case, warm disposition, and beaming smile. We would, in time, share many ups and downs. But that first day, Rob became familiar with my case and gave me a couple of light exercises to do plus a heat bag to use on my thigh. The bag was a great tool and gave me much-needed relief from the constant pain I was experiencing.

I visited Rob weekly for about six weeks. Every week, another stretch or exercise was added to my routine. He lent me a floor pedal machine that at first caused me a significant amount of discomfort but soon eased my knee pain. My knee had been injured in the accident. I had sustained a ruptured posterior medial ligament—I think that is what it was called—and it resulted in my knee being very stiff, sore, wobbly, and weak.

On top of all the other injuries I had, this was a surprise. The extent of the damage and its effect upon my leg recovery had not been evident to me until I began physio. It was a setback, but I was slowly improving. Leg flexibility was increasing, and the pedal machine was my best friend and worst enemy rolled into one.

My physio routine now took up an hour or so a day, and it frustrated Marise at times. We would need to go somewhere, and I would be in the middle of my routine. I know she knew I had to do the exercises, but maybe I was a bit anal about them. I knew the only way back was discipline and hard work, and both I could give. Just watch me go!

★ ★ ★

The insurance company at last offered us $1,800 compensation for our car. I was so bloody cranky. Admittedly, it was a seven-year-old car, but it was a great car—reliable and straight and clean. I contacted the insurance company and made my case to them. I told them of the situation Marise and I were in at the moment, with me incapacitated and Marise struggling to manage the farm and her work commitments. We would have to replace the car, as we had no other reliable transport and lived an hour from town. Even though I was basically housebound, I still had some fight in me and relished the opportunity to find some fairness.

To their credit, they revised the payment up to $2,800, which was no great improvement but did help us scratch the money together to purchase a second-hand 2007 Mazda Tribute from a lovely couple in Inverell for $7,000. We now again had a reliable vehicle, unlike the 1996 Holden Rodeo we used predominantly as a work vehicle.

I also fought a protracted battle with Australia Post in regard to us getting a mail delivery. We had never had a mailbox; our mail was delivered to Dad and Mum at Watsons Creek, ten kilometres away. Dad came out to the farm daily or thereabouts and so delivered our mail then. We decided to establish our own mailbox. Now, that should not have been too awkward, no it should not. But the ensuing three-month battle occupied my energies and fuelled my frustrations. Eventually, much to our delight and Dad's relief, our mail deliveries commenced, and another box of mine was ticked.

★ ★ ★

Week after week, I visited Rob. His cheerful demeanour and huge smile greeted me every time, and I was driven to do my best for him (and obviously for myself). The pain in my thigh remained ever-present and acute, and many Panadols were devoured to get me through the days and the physio visits. Going to town and physio involved a four-hour return trip. The day after these journeys were write-offs. The pain would be too debilitating to allow me to do anything more than lay around.

From day one, Marise had been insistent that my goals and expectations were a little (if not a damn sight) optimistic and that I would be basically incapacitated in the future. The matter of what I would do with my remaining productive years was one of conjecture. I was insistent that I would make a full recovery and eventually get back to where I had been a few months ago. Marise was far more realistic, and the girls were on board with her in most respects. I must admit, my expected full recovery was not entirely based on medical science. The doctors and specialists we were seeing were not prescribing to my theory wholeheartedly either.

There was discussion on whether I should go to TAFE and retrain for some farm-related occupation—maybe do a wool-classing course or the like, a job not as heavy on the body as shearing. I had always enjoyed photography and had been a wedding photographer since I was about sixteen. This was one avenue of work I could imagine turning my hand to on a more permanent basis, and Hannah had business cards printed up for me to drop off at businesses and hand out to people we knew. I entertained the prospect wholeheartedly, while all the time, harbouring my personal ambition to return to shearing, farm life, and work.

My resulting determination and drive to push on harder with the physio and exercises made me very single-minded in my outlook. The effort I was putting into my recovery was showing results, and with the steady improvement, my optimism rose.

Hannah and Jay bought me an exercise bike, and I began to use it on a regular basis while I watched television. It proved to be very beneficial and provided a good cardio workout also. I was feeling better about myself; my progress was pleasing to me. I was by now, daily, walking up and down our back veranda in my walker. This was slow and painful but, gradually, getting easier to manage. With more strength came more activity, which resulted in a little more independence. Onward and upward was the motto.

★ ★ ★

One of the many positives of my predicament revolved around going to town. Now this may seem strange. I was still getting about in a wheelchair, and this was problematic, particularly for Marise. Getting the chair in and out of the car, setting it up and extricating me from the car, and getting me into it was a big enough job in itself; add in wheeling me around where the terrain was steep or rough and putting up with my running commentary, and Marise was once again an angel.

I loved the supermarket, though, yes I did! Marise would give me a list of a couple of items, and I would trundle up and down the aisles, searching out my quarry. When I did locate my item, I was always assisted by a random shopper, particularly if the item was high on the shelving. There always seemed to be some dear soul who was only too happy to help, and I was always ever-so-grateful for the assistance.

As with many experiences postaccident, my faith in humanity was being bolstered with nearly every interaction I was having with random people. I was thriving on this aspect of my journey. Marise was not quite as excited about my newfound "big beautiful world full of wonderful people" theory and was mostly uncomfortable with me encouraging these random interactions and conversations with strangers we would come across in the process of our shopping trips.

By July, I had built up and strengthened my leg and knee enough that I could get around with the help of a crutch. This gave me a little more independence. I could now ride the quad bike and spend a little time riding around the property. Marise and the girls were once more a little concerned about my activities, but I was again insistent that I would be careful. Although I could, in reality, only manage short adventures, it all helped me reconnect with the day-to-day running of the farm. I could take the dogs for a run, open gates if needed, and be a little help to Marise—though in truth, I was still a liability and a worry, neither of which she needed at the time.

★ ★ ★

Another beautiful person entered my life at this stage: an English-born occupational therapist employed by RACQ. Her name was Lizzy Parsons, and her infectious laugh and warm smile brightened my world each day she visited. Lizzy came prepared. She had bought a pair of work boots to wander around the farm in as she watched and assisted me through the day-to-day activities of my farming life.

She assisted me onto the tractor to assess my ability to operate it. We looked at fencing and watched Marise perform sheep-drenching and associated procedures. Lizzy even assessed my ability to get on and off our quad bike. Inside the house, she checked out our bathroom, toilet, kitchen, and bedroom to see if any aids were needed for my safe function in and around the house.

Lizzy visited me half a dozen times over a six-month period, always so happy and obliging. She soon understood the dynamics of our farm, my present restrictions, and some future issues that might present themselves. I struggled through the experience, in much pain, but I was optimistic that the assessment would be the catalyst for assistance or treatment that could be beneficial in my recovery.

★ ★ ★

There was some hope on Marise's and my part that some monies might be available to us to employ someone to help around the farm, on a casual basis, to take the weight off Marise. This proved not to be the case. It was suggested that we keep a diary of all the farm-related activities completed by Marise, our girls, friends, or paid workers. There would possibly be some reimbursement to us for the work I could not perform at this stage and into the future.

The accident and my incapacity resulted in little of the necessary farm maintenance being achieved over the coming years. We had no money to employ casual workers, and it was not right that we expect family or friends to perform unpaid work for us when they had lives and commitments of their own. So Marise toiled on, working at the school and then coming home and working day after day, doing all she could manage to keep the farm going. We did still receive so much help from Dad, the girls, and other family members. Their assistance was received with heartfelt thanks. We were blessed by their generosity and will be forever grateful for their help through those first few years. I pushed on with such determination, irrespective of the pain, but I was becoming more frustrated with the progress.

I was starting to push myself a little harder than I should have. Limited independence was not enough for me, and so I started doing more and more—and often paid a heavy price for my exuberance. I could not always let on how much pain I was in. It would have done my situation no good at all, and my activities would have been curtailed considerably. So onward and upward was the motto, at home and at physio. Rob lifted the bar every visit. My progress was still pleasing, but the pain was always a concern to Rob. He felt that it should be easing faster than it was. Some exercises he set, I struggled with and found myself unable to achieve.

Marise and Dad were still the backbone of the farm. Garry and Graeme, Marise's brothers, came out and helped us shear in the spring. I hobbled about and helped, probably only getting in the way, but we made our way through the ewe shearing. I was able to shear one or two, though the weakness in my leg made the process awkward. By the time we had to shear the wethers and young sheep, I was able to do a few more and slowly improved from there. The stretching and the weight of the sheep was like a workout, and though followed by a day or two of pain, the benefits were pleasing.

★ ★ ★

September had been a special month for us. Hannah's and Sarah's birthdays were close together—the second and fourteenth, respectively—and my grandmother Connie's on the same day as Sarah's. Connie turned ninety-four, and all the family would be here for the party. It would be a wonderful weekend, and in fact most of it was. We partied and laughed so much, it was a real tonic. That weekend also marked the toughest day I'd had since the accident.

We were all together at home one evening, and it was the first time we'd all been together since the accident. We sat around the kitchen table, and ultimately the conversation turned to the accident. Till that day, we had not had the opportunity to discuss the ins and outs of the accident, and this was the debrief many of us needed so badly. As I write this, tears come to my eyes, even after seven years. We sat and individually recalled what we experienced and felt, what parts we played, and in what order the events of that day unfolded.

My heart broke that day, and never will I see those people in the same light. The pain in each of their stories was so raw and present. A few months had not been enough for the emotion to lessen. My dear Sarah's recollections left me in such a state I had to excuse myself, retire to the bedroom, and cry for half an hour or so.

★ ★ ★

Day by day, I was starting to feel as if I was contributing to the bigger picture at last, and I was ever keen to move forward. Marise was still not entirely on board and cautioned against doing anything that might cause damage. It had been seven months by now, and I insisted that I was all right. We once again made it through the shearing, with help from our workforce, and the tussle between Marise, the girls, and I continued, always around my activity. As per usual, I had to play down the pain, telling myself it was only normal in the recovery from an injury of this kind, but I still needed to call on painkillers on a regular basis to get through.

There are plenty of heavy jobs to be done on a farm—fencing and the like—and there was plenty of this building up. I started doing little bits and pieces of fence repair and tried to do a bit of work on the tractor, ploughing and the like. It didn't seem to matter, though; no matter how much exercise or increased activity I achieved, the pain in my leg did not lessen. There were obviously moments of self-doubt as to how full my recovery would be, and I had to continually push these to the back of my mind. But the pain was ever-present, as was my concern, and I struggled not to let either show outwardly—a hard ask when Marise and I were together 24/7.

I remember I spent a couple of weeks cleaning up a paddock for cropping. There were a few fallen trees on the block, and I cut them up and then stacked them to burn. Picking up, carrying, and throwing the timber on the heaps was heavy work, at least for me in my condition, but for a couple of hours a day, for a week or so, I felt alive, challenged, and worthy of a place in the grand scheme of things. Once more I was contributing to our farm and world. It felt great!

★ ★ ★

Christmas 2013 rolled around, and we were lucky to be the hosts that year. Our families took it in turns to host Christmas, and after the year we had just come through, it was a real treat to have everyone together for a great celebration of family and love. We all shared so much fun, playing tennis, cards, and various other activities that symbolised our Christmases. The three days our family was together for Christmas were wonderful.

Zoe had gained entry into Southern Cross University at the Lismore campus and would be starting there in mid-February. She was excited to be doing her degree in visual arts, though a little apprehensive about moving away from home. Sarah and Hannah had done their degrees, and masters, at the University of New England, only an hour from where we lived, but Zoe would be five hours away. To add to her stress level, Marise, Michelle, Paul, Mum, Dad, and I would be travelling to Bunburry, in Western

Australia, for the wedding of a cousin of ours from the Northern Territory. We would be leaving a couple of days before Zoe had to be in Lismore. She would have to pack up and leave without us being home to see her off, but we were looking forward to the trip to WA and assured her that all would be fine.

We flew out to Perth in late January. We were still in the grip of drought at home. Hannah, Zoe, and Jay would keep an eye on things for the two weeks we were away.

The ten days in WA were great. My leg pain was as always a hindrance, and once again I was up to my old tricks: physio activities every morning and afternoon, plus walking up and down every flight of stairs available. My pedantic behaviour was probably not appreciated by my travelling companions, though they rarely mentioned it. Dad occasionally asked why I kept it up. I could give no satisfactory explanation. Apparently, I was blindly ploughing on towards what I hoped would be satisfaction for me.

I tried to do all I could. We walked through caves, explored the beautiful coastline, saw amazing sunsets, and had an absolute ball of a time. If ever you get an opportunity to explore WA's south-west coast, or in fact any of that beautiful state, don't miss the chance. It is truly spectacular.

★ ★ ★

Sometime in February or March, Marise and I were required to see a doctor in Brisbane to assess our recoveries, postaccident, for insurance purposes. We once again trundled up the New England Highway to Brisbane, spent the night with Michelle and Paul, and then, the next morning, made our way into central Brisbane to see Dr. Pentas. After a short wait in his reception room, we were ushered into his consultation room and made his acquaintance.

The doctor took my hand, shook it heartily, and said he was happy to see me. I was a little shocked that he was genuinely delighted to see me, and I had to know why. I asked of him why the interest in me, and he proceeded to inform me that he rarely, if ever, met anyone like me. The fact of the matter was, anyone who had suffered the femur injuries I had invariably bled to death at the scene. The chance of my femur smashing as it had done and not tearing the arteries to shreds was remote, and I was an extremely fortunate soul.

Dr. Pentas gave Marise and I the once over. We thanked him and were duly on our way. As we left his offices and made our way from there to the train station, we chatted about the meeting, actually wondering about the waste of time—the drive up and back from Watsons Creek—for a half-hour consultation. We were pleased to have ticked the box and were naively imagining that the whole ordeal would be soon behind us. Now that the legal wheels were in motion, our matter would be finalised, and we would be able to get on with our lives.

Even as we strolled along on that bright, clear, muggy Brisbane morning, a weight rested uneasily upon me. The unlikeliness of my existence, the randomness of my survival, now posed the obvious question: how would I honour this good fortune and not squander this precious gift of a real second chance? I had no immediate answer to the question. It seemed a hell of a lot to get my head around. In fact, I could well have done without the entire revelation, but the question remained, like a line from a sixties Pink Floyd or Led Zeppelin song—a subliminal, subconscious, there-all-the-time question. It was a question that demanded an answer, one I knew I could not give until I possibly lay on my deathbed, hopefully many years from now, and reflected on my postaccident life, hoping I had indeed honoured the second chance offered to me and gratefully accepted in that mangled car on the freeway just north of Brisbane in 2013.

Many defining moments arise throughout the timeline of our existence, and coming to terms with and evaluating the significance of them requires much soul-searching and contemplation. I daily search for the strength and guidance to do all I can to help others, and my family, in their personal journeys. There are many days when my actions fall way short of my expectations and my time is selfishly given in the pursuit of material reward. Still, I try my best to put smiles on people's faces wherever I am and whatever I am doing. Hopefully, in some small way, I can make the world better—even one person's world, if only for a minute.

* * *

We returned home to much the same, and I went to see Rob at physio again, and we once more took up the road to recovery. Progress was still pleasing, though the long-standing hurdles remained in regard to my thigh. By April, Rob was concerned that I still had such leg pain and sent me to see Dr. Diebold for a check-up. The doctor examined me and sent me off for X-rays. We made an appointment to see him again in the afternoon to discuss the X-rays and such. Marise and I had lunch and did a couple of jobs around Armidale before returning for our afternoon appointment.

When we were seated, Dr. Diebold brought up the images and, to our surprise, revealed that my femur had not healed. A callous had formed over the break, but the bones had not formed a successful union. This was pretty shattering news for us, and I was once more thrown into an unpleasant situation where I was no longer in control. I hated these times. Riding a roller coaster of emotion and frustration, at the mercy of doctors, insurance companies, and lawyers—it was not a ride to my liking.

Dr. Diebold offered to perform the surgery to reunite my femur, and I politely declined. I asked him if he knew of a surgeon he could recommend to me. He made a few calls and then referred me to Dr. Doug King in Brisbane. The operation would involve the removal of the titanium nail that ran through the length of my femur. The bone would have to be drilled out to give the best chance of a successful healing, and a replacement nail would be inserted.

I was horrified, to say the least. This was the last thing I wanted and needed, but there was no option. The renailing was critical; there was a chance of the current nail fracturing down the track if the femur hadn't healed. So I had to jump on the roller coaster, hold on tight, and pray to God that all would be fine.

Now I must admit, I'd had doubts about my leg. In particular, one of the exercises I was given by Rob involved laying on my belly, bending my right leg, and letting it rotate to the side to stretch my hip joint and muscles. The funny thing, if I can call it funny, was that when I did this exercise, I could feel and hear the bones grating ever so slightly in my thigh. Up till now, though, with everyone saying that my leg was healed, there seemed little point in taking much notice. Now I felt very vulnerable and was pretty concerned about doing the right thing.

6. Off to Surgery Again

I contacted Dr. King and made an appointment for April 22, in three weeks' time. The days ticked on towards the appointment, and my nerves were frayed. The prospect of another surgery was not one I awaited joyously. I had not sat in a car for an extended period as of yet and did not relish the trip at all.

Marise and I had gone down the coast to Foster in early April, and we drove up to Taree one morning. It had been the first time I had sat in a car in highway traffic since the accident. I was petrified. With every car that came towards us, I winced. I was near panic-stricken by the time we arrived in Taree. The wounds from the accident were still raw. It is strange, the workings of the human mind. There was no logic to my fear, and I would have to learn to tame it.

We drove to Lismore on April 20. Sarah came with us, and we eventually found Zoe's house and stayed the night there. We had a tour of Lismore and the Uni the next morning, then in the afternoon, Marise, Sarah, and I went on to Brisbane and stayed the night at Michelle and Paul's. It was nice to catch up with them. It was because they lived in Brisbane that we'd decided that I would have my operation there, so I could convalesce at their house a couple of days after I was discharged from hospital. After a quiet morning, we made our way into Brisbane and met Dr. King. I have never felt so at ease with a doctor. His manner was reassuring, and he listened to my story and any questions I had. Apparently, he had trained as a vet before training as an orthopaedic surgeon. He obviously had a way with animals, and so we hit it off immediately.

He scheduled the operation for May 29 and went through the entire procedure with us. We left still feeling nervous, but confident in our choice of surgeon. We had about six weeks till the operation, so we sat back and waited—not only for the op but for the insurance company to sign off on it.

D-Day came ever closer, and finally RACQ announced that they would pay for the surgeon and hospital but not the anaesthetist. We were contemplating the prospect of having to pay for the anaesthetist ourselves and had actually resigned ourselves to the fact with one day left till the op, RACQ having still not signed off. This was very frustrating and highly unprofessional of them. We lived seven hours away from Brisbane, and it wasn't till the morning of the 28th, the day we had to leave, that they eventually gave the OK. We had been frantic up till then, trying to organise the finances to pay for the op. It was extremely stressful. It was the first but the not last time RACQ would put us in a stressful situation. Thanks, RACQ!

★ ★ ★

We stayed the night at Michelle and Paul's before heading off at about six o'clock for Greenslopes Hospital, twenty minutes away, for the pre-op and such. There were many delays that day, and it was not until about two o'clock that I was prepped for the operation. I was wheeled into a room beside an operating theatre and set up for surgery. Doug drew lines and arrows on my thigh so they didn't pin my leg on the wrong way, then he gave me the pre-op anaesthetic. I was then wheeled into the theatre and placed on the operating table.

There was music playing in the operating theatre, and it was Hank Williams singing "I'm So Lonesome I Could Cry." Apparently Doug or someone else in the theatre enjoyed early country music, as I did, so it was quite relaxing. Before I nodded off, Doug asked if I was all right. I said yes and told him to have fun. He gave a little laugh, and that was all she wrote. I was gone.

There were many questions I had asked myself over the twelve months since the accident, and a few of them I hoped would be answered today. Would I have a similar experience after the operation, in regard to the computer program experience or the terrorist kidnapping experience? Both were related to the immediate aftermath of the accident, but there were no dramas with this operation or post-op—no weird dreams. So those questions remain and make me wonder to this day.

It was about eight o'clock before I came to in the ward, well past dinner, and as I had not eaten for twenty-four hours, Marise organised the nurses to find me something to eat. I can see why they would not ask before the op if I would like dinner that evening. The variances of operations and not knowing if I would feel like eating are understandable. But surely some means of sustenance would be readily available given the circumstances. Instead, it seemed as if a few nurses had to chip into their own dinners to feed me. If such was the case, I am in debt to their generosity and thoughtfulness.

In grogginess, I ate a little and dozed off quite soon afterwards, leaving Marise to drive back to Michelle's in the darkness. Marise is not at all comfortable driving in cities, and even less at night, but she managed without incident, and drove back and forth the next few days till my discharge.

★ ★ ★

The renailing was far less intrusive than the original operation had been, so apart from the obvious pain, recovery was relatively quick. The three days in hospital were followed by a couple of days at Michelle and Paul's, and I was grateful for them particularly. I was by then in far less pain and ready to undertake the seven-hour drive home.

There was one difference in regard to my treatment after this operation. I would have to give myself heparin injections for about three weeks to reduce the risk of blood-clotting. Prior to the accident, I'd had a bit of a phobia in regard to needles, and in my youth I'd had a few embarrassing episodes when, as a bulletproof twenty-odd-year-old, I nearly fainted after having blood taken for pathology tests. I now felt real sympathy for those people who have to give themselves injections for whatever reason. After three weeks, I was certainly glad to see the last of those needles. The lovely nurse who instructed me in the administration was extremely gentle, and her method proved to be painless and efficient. It did make the three weeks go a little easier.

We arrived home once more to a winter chill, and it took a few weeks of sitting on the lounge in front of our warming wood heater, reading and watching TV, before I could get around on crutches again. This setback did little to improve my mental health, and as such all the associated feelings of uselessness once more swept over me. There were many teary moments and crying in Marise's arms as she once more took me by the hand and, like an angel, led me through the tough times.

The next few months, I took it very easy. There was still pain in my thigh, but all indications were pointing to a successful result—one I, and we, needed and desired. This time, no stone would remain unturned. Doug insisted that we drive to Brisbane every six weeks for the first three months, which was quite onerous. But we managed, often driving up one day and home the next. The X-rays and scans all looked fine, and we at last viewed the future with optimism.

★ ★ ★

Sarah and Mathew had mentioned their desire to get married late in 2013 and had set their wedding date for October 3, 2014. They had been reticent to approach us, given our financial situation and my health, but we had reassured them that there was no way any of our difficulties would interfere with their marriage. So for the next few months, it was all systems go.

I was once more driven to recovery. It seemed there was never a time in my journey when I really relaxed from physio or exercise. There was always a goal. Now I had to build up enough to dance at my dear sweet girl's wedding, and I let nothing stand in my way. The deadline was to be tight, and there were moments when there seemed real doubt as to how capable I would be on the day, but it was all coming together.

By the wedding day, all was well. We had managed through the arrangements, though Sarah and Mathew had done 90 per cent of the organising. The wedding was delightful, the day was beautiful, and all the family was together. Dad was in great form, and it was so special to have him there with us on that special day. Sarah and Mathew were truly blessed, as were we all. It was a wondrous day, and one we will never forget. I danced with my dear girl at the reception—not very sprightly, but without the need of a crutch or walking stick. That was never even a remote possibility. All was well in the world—for now, anyway.

★ ★ ★

On October 31, our nephew Danny, niece Emily, and Emily's boyfriend, Jack, were involved in a car accident only ten kilometres from our home. Our telephone was out of order that night, and fortunately so. I was captain of the Watsons Creek rural fire brigade; the local command centre in Tamworth had tried to phone us to attend the accident but was unable to make contact with us. Jack had walked three kilometres to raise the alarm and find help, which he managed to somehow do despite his injuries. We did not hear of the accident till the next morning. I know we would have responded to the accident if we had been contactable, but I fear, given the rawness still shadowing me, I might have been too distraught to be of any assistance.

As it was, the terrible injuries and distress suffered by the very-lucky-to-be-alive people involved proved hard for me to handle, and many teary days ensued. Danny and Jack had nasty injuries but were up and about quite soon. Emily's condition was far more serious. She sustained a broken hip, broken pelvis, torn liver, damaged kidney, and severe head injury. She was kept in an induced coma for about a week, and it would take her three years of hard work and treatment before she made a complete recovery.

The one tiny positive we shared was the opportunity to recover together, and we were able to give each other tremendous support and help. We caught up on a regular basis at family get-togethers, birthdays, and the like, and we now share a little common story—not the most spectacular or exciting story, but an adventure nonetheless. We were blessed in the fact that all three made complete recoveries, and at the moment, all are well, best friends, and most precious members of our family.

★ ★ ★

As the year 2014 came to an end, my leg was getting stronger, but there was still pain. No matter what exercises I did or how hard I worked on it, the pain never subsided. I was continuing to see Dr. King on a regular basis, and he was happy with the progress, though unsure about the cause of the pain.

I had begun to wonder about the pain myself. Was it, in fact, not really there but purely in my head? I really did wonder.

Everyone was quite sure that my leg had healed and that I should have moved past the painful period, so although neither Dr. King nor my physio, Rob, ever implied that it could all be in my head, I did wonder myself.

As the new year unfolded, I pushed myself more than I had before. I started shearing a little more—a day here, a day there—and tried to work through the pain and discomfort. I cannot put into words the pain I went through. I could manage to shear till lunchtime, but after the lunch break, the pain was horrid and only increased as the afternoon progressed. By five o'clock, knock-off time, I had a job to walk, and getting in and out of a car was very awkward.

I pushed on, though, convinced that the more I worked, the sooner I would build up my leg and ease the pain. But it seemed that no amount of work could do the job. I would awake the next morning to head off to work barely able to use my right leg. After it warmed up a bit, it was manageable once more till lunch, then downhill once again. Marise despaired at my predicament, but we battled on together towards a common goal: recovery and getting on with our lives.

Marise was still teaching at the Kingstown Public School two or three days a week, and those days for me were sometimes a little easier, though there were still many day-to-day jobs that needed doing. Marise was working to keep our finances afloat, and it was really tough on her. Her days off were flat-out helping me, preparing programs, and marking schoolwork—duties she felt passionate about. It was hard for me to watch her working so hard, and I felt lousy being unable to give much assistance to our finances. There were some fairly low days for me as I tried my best to contribute in any way I could.

I was struggling mentally, and the effects on my life and well-being were diverse and many. My self-confidence was very low. I felt inadequate as a husband, father, farmer, and provider. As a result of these feelings, and the fears that accompanied them, I was suffering with intermittent impotence. My lack of self-worth made me self-conscious, and as a result I began to struggle in bed. The horrible thing about these eventualities is that your feelings of being inadequate are only fuelled to further lows by every continuing failure. Marise was so very understanding and assured me that it did not matter, but you can only imagine the despair I felt through these times.

I struggled with the ever-present farm conversation with mates and colleagues, as I was struggling to do much of the farm work and once again felt inadequate. I had lost my spark for life and was, in that respect, failing as a father, or felt that I was. I was losing my patience, and more often than not, Dad became the victim of this. Not that I was overly sharp or nasty to him, but I didn't have the patience to have the wonderful conversations I wish I'd had over that couple-of-year period.

I visited a psychologist a couple of times during that year to try to get my head around the changes I was going through. It was very helpful to me. He helped me understand my feelings and gave me a few coping mechanisms to help me work through troubling times and situations. The mindfulness techniques were very helpful, and I have used them many times over the years since.

★ ★ ★

Physio continued on. I saw Rob every few months and Dr. King a few times during the year also. The insurance side of the accident was starting to get a roll on, with phone calls and discussion. There was a feeling that my condition was stabilising, and so the process to finalise the case was gathering steam. I was apprehensive, though. There were still the couple of problems I was having—notably my leg pain, and my right arm had not been great postaccident.

It is funny, but my other injuries from the accident had never satisfactorily stabilised for me either. They'd had little attention, as attention had been predominantly focussed on my leg, but I had a continuous numbness in the big toe quadrant of my left foot, which was annoying, and my right arm ached and was extremely sensitive on the lower outside of my forearm, where it was plated. I could not rest my arm on a table, for example, or the pain would make me feel sick. Also, my arm ached after activity, and ached terribly after driving thirty minutes or so. I was not at all happy about the prospect of dealing with it postsettlement. I wanted it fixed before we reached that point.

I approached my family doctor in Uralla, and he got the ball rolling. He agreed that the plate should be removed in an attempt to alleviate pain and discomfort. He referred me to a surgeon in Tamworth, Dr. Wainright, and RACQ agreed to the operation.

I visited Dr. Wainright on October 6, and after examining me, he agreed to remove the plate. He would do the operation on December 13, with RACQ on board again. I was excited about maybe relieving the pain but definitely about removing that bloody plate.

We would be having Christmas at Mum's and Dad's at Watsons Creek, and we would have to do a fair bit of work there to help them prepare. With my op so close to Christmas, we would have to get the jobs done beforehand, so things were pretty hectic leading up to the op. I was looking forward to being able to have a couple of quiet weeks leading up to Christmas post-op.

Dr. Wainright would do the operation as day surgery. I had to be at Tamarra, the private hospital in Tamworth, at about six in the morning, and as always had a considerable wait till about eleven o'clock when I was finally into surgery. Marise went down the street to do some grocery shopping while I was in surgery and was back at the hospital by about six in the evening, when I was discharged.

We headed home, and I must confess, it was the sickest I have ever felt. At no time—trapped in the car, coming to, after the initial surgeries, after the subsequent renailing, or at any other time have I felt so horribly unwell. The trip home was an ordeal I hope never to have to repeat. We arrived home, and I crawled into bed. Thankfully, I awoke the next morning feeling alive and much improved.

★ ★ ★

The next few weeks, I kept fairly quiet. Christmas came and went—once again a wondrous occasion. I am such a Christmas person; I really do love it.

By mid-January, I was back at it again. We finished off our shearing, pressed up the wool, and battled through the summer's heat. My arm was a little better, and with the promise of more improvement in that area, I was a happier soul.

By this stage, the general consensus in regard to my leg was that it was healed and now only required strengthening. I had not seen Rob for a few months, and apart from the occasional call from RACQ in regard to my condition and an also occasional call from my lawyers, I and we were battling on. We had now slipped back into drought, which had been drifting in and out since 2013, before the accident. Once more in its grip, we carted water and fodder in an attempt to keep our stock in good-enough condition to get them through the winter. It was tough, and draining on our financial, mental, and physical resources. My leg still hindered my ability to manage the demands required to do the day-to-day work.

Marise had given her notice at the Kingstown Public School, where she had taught part-time since 2003. She had decided that the demands of the farm were too much for me and so chose to give up work before school returned for the 2016 year. It was a tough call for Marise to make. We were, as I have said, tipping back towards drought, but she was concerned for my health, physical and mental, and so made the move. We were committed to the farm, and eventually it would have to stand on its own two feet, without our supplementing it. Zoe was established at Lismore, well into her degree in visual arts, and so we were pretty well only responsible for our own world, apart from the occasional hand we gave Zoe.

Our world had settled considerably. The surgery on my forearm had been successful, and it seemed as if things were improving. My leg strengthened more. It was amazing how slow the strength came back, but underlying this steady improvement was constant pain. There seemed no getting away from it, and once again there were doubts in my mind as to its origin.

Since the accident, where my thigh muscles had been considerably damaged by the broken femur tearing through it, the front of my thigh had been very tight and hard. The muscles had been damaged so severely, it had been hard to soften then and get them working properly. The physio had been very helpful, and Rob had done a wonderful job, but the thigh was still as hard as a rock.

As the femur had healed at last, the pain could be attributed the thigh muscles, my head, or both. I told myself that it was purely physiological and that I could not possible generate such pain from thoughts alone, but still the doubt remained. There seemed little choice but to forge on, oblivious to the pain, in the hope of eventually improving the thigh muscles and hopefully relieving the pain.

I began doing a little shearing again, with little real improvement from previous attempts. I could still only manage a day or two at a time, with the same associated pain. But I was confident that the more I tried, the sooner the strength would return and the pain disappear.

Marise and I pushed on. The drought was once more taking its toll on our resources. Dry periods in the autumn are doubly brutal, as the grass that disappears will not grow again until well into the spring. This means that you are in for a very hard winter of feeding stock and possibly carting water. As the days passed by, the situation only worsened. Our predicament, as it had been since the accident, was ordinary. We would do the best we could.

★ ★ ★

In early May, Mum, my sisters Michelle and Debbie, and our first cousin Jacquie went on a vacation to Europe for three weeks. Dad had not wanted to travel; it was not his thing. Mum had pestered him for far too long that eventually she took it on herself; enlisted the assistance of Michelle, who worked in the travel business; rounded up Debbie and Jacquie; and headed off. Dad was not one bit concerned, wished them well, and probably looked forward to enjoying his own company for a while.

Dad visited us daily, as always, and was in great form. He helped me build a fence, and we spent some wonderful days together. Little did we know, they would be the last we would share.

A few days later, Dad decided to mow his lawn; at that time of year, it was really unnecessary, but he said it needed a tidy-up. While in the process, he managed to get his ride-on lawnmower stuck in a hole, and while attempting to pull it out, he broke a rib. Dad told me of the incident and said that his ribs were sore, but he was fine. He would give it a few days and see if it improved before seeing a doctor if necessary.

Three or four days later, with little improvement, he decided that he should go to the outpatients at Manilla. My niece took Dad to the Manilla hospital, where he was admitted, much to his disgust, and tests and examinations were carried out.

Dad's condition worsened, and by the time Mum returned from Europe, he had been transferred to Tamworth Base Hospital. Somewhere, somehow, the report from Manilla Hospital had been lost or misplaced, and the doctors at Tamworth, unaware that Dad had had the lawnmower incident, were treating him for a probable chest tumour.

Over the next week, Dad's condition deteriorated. Eventually, they realised that he in fact had a broken rib, which had resulted in him having a significant bruise that had become infected. He had by then developed blood poisoning.

He underwent a couple of operations in an attempt to clean up the infection, but to no avail. After a couple of weeks in hospital, he sadly passed away. If only he had been prescribed antibiotics at the start, he might well have survived the ordeal, but that was not to be the case.

I was obviously deeply hurt by his passing and felt aggrieved that our accident, and my recovery, had weighed heavily upon him. The added work and strain he had been placed under had robbed him of a few easier years and possibly more quality time with Mum.

Dad and I had spent pretty well every day of our working lives together. We had shorn together, and worked on the farm together, from when I was sixteen. We were so very close. It was awkward at times to have conversations, because we knew each other so very well. I still needed Dad's input, though I managed the farm pretty much myself.

His loss was multidimensional. I had lost a father, a mate, and a colleague, all while battling through the aftermath of the accident. I wasn't that fun person Dad knew those last couple of years, and I know he missed that and felt sad for me. As I have said previously, I felt guilty and responsible for many things postaccident. I wish I had have been able to tell Dad that I was going to be OK, something I never had a chance to tell him. In fact, I did not think at the time, during those last few days with him, that it was something that needed to be said. But on reflection, it did need to be said, and it was not. Sorry, Dad.

★ ★ ★

It began to rain shortly after Dad's death, and it rained and rained. It had rarely been as wet as it was in those winter months, and by early spring, our situation had improved markedly. It was quite a nice turn of events. The seasons rolled by. I was still doing a day or so of shearing from time to time, with similar pain. There seemed to be no improvement, regardless of the effort I put in.

I saw Dr. King in late 2016. He was happy with my progress but still flustered by the pain, so sent me for a CAT scan, the results of which we were not told, as we left Brisbane as soon as the scans were taken. As per normal, we puttered our way back down the highway, giving little thought to the visit or consultation.

In December, we had a meeting with my lawyer in Brisbane in regard to getting the ball rolling as far as compensation was concerned. I was happy that things were moving forward, but there was one worry for me. Everyone involved in the case—RACQ, Dr. King, my lawyers, and I—had been waiting for my condition to become stable and satisfactory before there could be any finalisation to the case. The lawyers were under the impression that all was relatively fine and that I had in fact reached a point where my condition was stable and satisfactory. I still had doubts and voiced my opinion, more than once, in the course of the meeting.

I inquired if the lawyers had received a report in regard to the CAT scan taken a few weeks before. They said they had not had any word in this regard, which was a little surprising to me. I said I would contact Dr. King on my return home and see if he could get a copy of the report sent to me and the lawyers.

Dr. King was on holidays after Christmas. I contacted his practice in early February to ask if the report from the CAT scan could be forwarded to me and the lawyers. Yes, that would be fine, they said. Consider it done.

As per normal, our world bumped along. We had slipped into a routine by now—me dealing with the pain and Marise giving me the latitude to take it easy whenever I needed a break. There seemed a real possibility that the insurance case would be finalised and I would just have to live with the consequences. I was only fifty-four, with, I had hoped, many more productive years ahead of me, but in reality I was seeing a steady decline in my condition, to the point of near incapacity, in regard to the farm work.

I felt as if my productive days were well and truly numbered, and it was a frightening prospect. I had many uncles who had continued shearing into their seventies, and I had always imagined I could have had a similar longevity. But my body was saying no, and regardless of what I'd hoped, my body would have the final say.

★ ★ ★

Early one bright February morning, the telephone rang at about six o'clock. This was a tad peculiar. Marise had gone to work, and I jumped out of bed to take the call. To my surprise, it was Dr. King. I questioned his early call, and he asked if I was sitting down. I was taken aback by the question but sat down all the same.

Doug went on to say that he had looked at the CAT scans that had been taken of my femur last December, and it was evident that the femur had not healed as yet, and that it was extremely unlikely that it would from here on without further surgery. By this stage, I was pleased that I was indeed sitting down. I asked what the alternatives were, and he quite frankly said that if the femur was left as it was, there was a distinct chance that one day the titanium rod would break, and since the bone was not strong enough to support itself, my leg would fracture again. There would then be the possibility of the broken bone severing an artery, and me bleeding to death.

In his opinion, there was little alternative left to me but to have another procedure, to renail and hopefully reunite the bone successfully. He left me to think about it. I knew full well that there was no alternative, but I needed a day or two to get my head around it.

Thankfully, Zoe was home for a couple of days. I woke her up and cried on her shoulder for a long while before returning to bed in an attempt to make the whole thing disappear. It was a terrible day. I was once again shattered, my world spinning out of control, my months of hard work at physio, pushing myself day after day in an attempt to strengthen my leg, the pain I had gone through, trying to return to shearing—now all to no avail and useless.

Shearing is a different sort of profession. The person who owns the sheep arranges, either personally or through a contractor, to have the sheep shorn, organising a number of shearers and associated staff to handle the wool. Quite often, if the sheep are ewes, close to lambing, there is a general rush to get the job done quickly and efficiently. Because of my condition, I was not always available, particularly if the shearing was to last any more than a couple of days, so I think I gained a reputation for being only a fill-in shearer, and not that reliable even in that capacity. It was not how I wanted to be seen. I felt horrible about the situation, and now once again, I would have to start all over, if in fact I chose to do so.

I was in a bad way. I didn't know if I could go through the whole process again. I didn't want to go through it again, and possibly again, and possibly again. For a fleeting moment, I contemplated having the leg amputated, in an attempt to sort out the whole damn thing once and for all, but that didn't last long.

I considered such thought unproductive, at the moment, given the circumstances.

When Marise came home from work that evening, we sat and discussed the situation in depth, both knowing there was no other choice than to go ahead with the surgery. I would ring Doug back the next day and confirm my willingness to go once again.

★ ★ ★

There was another aspect to the present dilemma I found myself in. A cousin of mine had had a similar accident, and two subsequent femoral nailings had failed to reunite the break. In the end, her doctor had had to remove the nail, place her in plaster, and hope the femur then healed. In the back of my mind, this seeded a fear that I might also have to go down this path.

The uncertainty of the whole thing was horrid. It played out on my mind constantly. I couldn't let Marise or the girls know about the torture I was going through; they had enough to deal with. So I put on a brave face and once again ploughed ahead.

I was feeling violated. Twice I had been told my leg had healed. I had gone through the ups and downs of recovery, physio, and all that, but in my heart the worst thing was the shearing. The pain I had put up with every day I had tried to get back into shearing had been excruciating. In hindsight, it might have been easier to just give up on the thought of shearing—just say, "No! The pain is too much!"—but I liken it to giving up smoking. Until you reach that point where you yourself decide to stop, it is pointless to try.

Now I am certainly not comparing shearing to smoking, but shearing was such a big part of my world. The social aspect of it was so enjoyable to me—catching up with mates and making new ones. There is a real comradery amongst shearers. The job is extremely tough, and everyone knows all too well the pain and suffering we each go through daily. There is a real appreciation of the effort we put in.

I once read an article where a doctor had studied shearers and concluded that shearing two hundred sheep in a day was equivalent to running a marathon in regard to physical exertion. For quite a few shearers, this amount of daily exertion is commonplace. Just put that into perspective—running five marathons a week, week after week.

It's a bloody tough job, and as I said, we really feel as if we belong to a club, and a pretty exclusive one to boot! As of yet, I was not ready to hang up my boots. I still held on to the dream of a return to the game, and twice already my hopes had been dashed into a crumbling, painful heap. Could I go through that again? I hoped so, but time was ticking, and my resolve was being tested, surely.

I had rang Doug and said I was good for a go. He assured me that this was the only way and asked when I would be able to have the surgery. Marise and I had gone through the ins and outs of the whole thing and decided that, if possible, mid-July would suit us. That would give us time to get a few things under control on the farm, and our workload in winter was lighter. It was not until spring that things tended to get hectic.

Once more, there would be added pressure in regard to my recovery. Hannah and Jay would be wed in early October, and so a July surgery would hopefully give me time to recover enough to walk my dear sweet girl down the aisle and dance with her at the wedding. We did have such a hectic life, but, oh how joyous in those respects.

7. Once More into the Breach, Dear Friend, Once More!

By early July, we were ready and had most things under control enough to have the week or so free for my operation. On July 16, Marise and I drove to Brisbane again. We were becoming quite familiar with the trek. We were booked in at a hotel in Woolloongabba, where we would stay the night. The next day, we had an eight o'clock start at the hospital for X-rays and pre-op procedures, and finding out where we would need to be early the next morning.

That evening, we found ourselves a lovely little Chinese restaurant and enjoyed a very tasty meal. It was just what I needed to take my mind off the day to come. Zoe would drive up to Brisbane from Lismore the next day and spend the few days with Marise. I was far happier knowing Zoe would be there for Marise. She would be Marise's chauffer for the few days.

Because the traffic was so busy around the hospital, Marise and I chose to walk to there the next morning at five thirty. We walked primarily because Marise did not feel confident about driving back to the hotel by herself. We had a lovely stroll through the city streets. It is amazing how many different lives cities have—their morning, day, evening, and night lives all distinctly different. Our predawn stroll was quite enjoyable. We took in all the peculiarities of the last vestiges of the night: patrons outside bars, coffee shops, yawning and waking, newspaper deliveries, and nurses and doctors making their way to the hospital, where we were also destined.

I imagine that in the back of most people's minds before going into surgery is the distant, niggling fear that all may not go well, and that was the case for me that morning. Marise and I walked hand in hand, me occasionally saying things she need not hear and her reassuring me, but mainly in love, and so very grateful for each other and the company on this cool Brisbane morning.

We arrived a little before six in the morning and sat in the foyer for about an hour till we were ushered into the pre-op suite, where I was prepared for surgery. After being shaved from below the waist to below my right knee, I was painted from the middle of my back to below the knee with a pink solution. Then a sticky film was stuck all over the prepared area. The preparations were different from the last surgery—mainly because this time, the operation would be more invasive.

The previous renailing had been done through an incision made above my hip, but this time, to hopefully accomplish a satisfactory result, not only would the nail be replaced but my femur would be broken and cleaned, and a hormone treatment would be placed in and around the bone to assist in healing. For this reason, a significant incision would have to be made through my thigh, adjacent to the break, and another above my knee, to remove the old securing screws and then secure the new nail after implanting. As before, there would be a significant incision above my hip to allow the removal and reinsertion of the new nail.

So eventually, I was all painted and plastered and ready for surgery. This time, sadly, there was none of the theatre that had preceded the previous renailing; no little chat, no music. I was anaesthetised in the ward and can just recall being wheeled out of the room, after saying goodbye to Marise.

The operation went well. I am only going on Doug's word; I was sound asleep throughout. But there was a little hiccup. A component used in drilling the bone out disintegrated during the operation, and little bits of it flew everywhere. The clean-up of the shrapnel from inside my leg, and the manual drilling of the bones because another component was not available, meant the operation went seven hours instead of about three. Doug was happy, though. He said he had never heard of this piece of equipment failing before, so once again, I seemed the catalyst for one-offs!

It was early the next morning before I remember anything. My first conscious thought was, *What have I done?* I was in such pain—much more than I'd had at any other point. Marise and Zoe were with me all day. It must have been deadly boring for them; I can't imagine I was much fun to be around. They must have kept each other company. The next day, they went to the botanical gardens, an outing they both enjoyed immensely. I was happy to be left to my own devices for the day. It gave me a chance to brighten up, get a couple of good sleeps, and get on top of the pain.

By the next day, I was feeling much better, and Marise and Zoe and I had a more interesting day together. By day three, there was an inkling of my discharge. I objected. I knew I was in no state to be released yet. Common sense was eventually seen, and I was allowed to stay another day, much to my relief.

The next morning, I was discharged. I was able to manoeuvre about a little on crutches. I was fairly wobbly, but with assistance, I managed to get into the car. Zoe drove us back to Michelle's, where I settled into life on Michelle's lounge. I spent the next couple of days on it. I slept there, ate there, and watched television from there. It was extremely comfortable and warm. I was steadily improving, which was needed. We would have to be home for Marise to go to work on the 24th.

★ ★ ★

One other thing was troubling me and causing considerable discomfort. I was suffering from a terrible itching radiating from beneath the dressings, covering the considerable wounds resulting from the surgery. The pain made it particularly uncomfortable to lie on my back, and it wasn't until the dressings were removed a week later that the reason for the itch became obvious. I'd had an allergic reaction to the pink solution used to disinfect my leg and hip, and under the dressing, when removed, Marise discovered several large blisters. One in particular, on my hip, was the size of the palm of my hand.

The blisters took a couple of weeks to settle down. They seemed to just add another dimension to the unfolding adventure. This journey I was on just kept giving and giving, always with a surprise around the next corner. I just hoped and prayed there were not too many more corners before me on the road to recovery.

★ ★ ★

Marise drove me home on the 23rd. We left Michelle's at nine thirty in the morning, the same time Zoe headed back to Lismore. We were so very grateful for her assistance in our hour of need. We had a very steady trip, with couple of stops apart from lunch and a toilet break. I needed to get out of the car and stretch a couple of times. We were home by seven that evening. Thankfully, my cousin Greg had been able to keep an eye on the place while we were away, feeding the dogs and so on, and he had our wood heater going nicely so that the house was cosy on our return.

Marise went off to work the next day, and I once again settled into life on our lounge, where I would stay for the next couple of weeks. I was on strict orders to do nothing for a couple of months. This time, my leg had to heal. There was no going back again, so I put my feet up and followed doctor's orders.

Marise, and at times the girls, once more took on the work required. The drought had taken up anew, and the demands on them grew daily. Garry and Graeme, Marise's brothers, and Garry's son Danny were wonderful. They came over when required, crutching and shearing sheep to help us out. For one little mob of fifty-four sheep, Marise was insistent that we would not bother anyone, and she proceeded to crutch them herself. This was an enormous effort on her part. It took her half a day, but she persevered, and lo and behold, she managed to get them done.

Marise's knowledge of farm management and her self-confidence grew over the years postaccident. She became a more independent, resilient, determined person. To say that she thrived on the experience might be taking it a bit too far, but the need to keep things going, her unwavering support for me, and her commitment to the farm drove her to new heights, achieving things she had never dreamed possible for herself. We both grew as individuals and as a couple as a result of the accident. As they say, "It is an ill wind that blows no good!"

★ ★ ★

The next few months saw regular visits to Dr. King, and more X-rays to verify the healing of the femur. All seemed to be going well, but we had been here before. I was still a little apprehensive. It wasn't easy to accept the fact that this time, all would be fine. I couldn't let the good news go to my head. I had to stay off my leg for as long as necessary. I hobbled around on crutches again, well and truly over them by now. The one step forward and two steps back was draining, physically and emotionally.

We counted down to Hannah and Jay's wedding. All the arrangements were coming along nicely. Hannah wanted to have the ceremony on the top of a mountain behind Watsons Creek that held a very special place in all of our hearts. The logistics of arranging transport of the guests, tables, chairs, and all the wedding bits and pieces up an eight-kilometre four-wheel-drive track were daunting, but doable for us. I was desperately wanting to be more involved, but I had to take a back seat in most work-related respects. I did everything I could, including painting chairs, tables, and stools.

The day arrived, and everything went to plan. I took the wedding photos for Hannah and Jay, as I had done for Sarah and Mathew. It was something I could do for them—just a special little gift from me. It meant the day was rather big for me, as it was for all involved, but I really loved taking a bit bigger role in the proceedings and was, as always, so very proud of my family.

Fortunately, I had reached a point where I could get around without the aid of crutches. Though my walking was still hindered and I had a discernible limp, I managed to get through the day and dance with my dear sweet girl, and my darling Marise, to celebrate the day. We had an absolute ball. It was great to be alive, and I was alive.

Regardless of what the past few years had thrown at us, and in particular me, I had never lost my zest for life. I had always found such joy in my family and the world. The ups and downs were just a part of the journey that anyone going through a similar situation would endure, not to be pondered on for the rest of your life but to be worked through, step by step, till you had come to terms with it, accepted it, and moved on. I was hoping that point was just around the corner for me now.

8. THE FINAL LEG

I eventually returned to physiotherapy. I hope Rob was happy to see me again; I was happy to be once more under his care. We settled into the routine of exercises and stretches. This was round three for us, a battle-hardened team. Rob's professional guidance and approach, and my determination, would surely lead me to the holy grail of my journey: full use and strength in my leg.

I began walking up and down our road—well, *hobbling* would be the more appropriate description. Since the accident, I had walked with my right foot turned outward. This would apparently lead to hip problems (just what I needed) unless I managed to turn my foot inward. I can't tell you how difficult it is to consciously will yourself, with every step you take, to physically turn your foot in. Trying to focus on this one thing thousands of times a day eventually does your head in. My pedantic nature only made the ordeal more consuming.

I had been doing this since I started to walk after the accident, and now, five years later, here I was, still trying to get these muscles and ligaments to either stretch or loosen, to enable my leg to swing in an anatomically correct arc. I studied my foot marks in the sand after walking without trying consciously to turn my toes inward, and I would always be frustrated by the sight of the left foot tracking straight, the right foot pointing out towards God knows where. So on and on I pushed.

Now seven years on, I hope there is a little improvement. Well, I'm sure there is, but it is still far from perfect. I must confess, 90 per cent of the time I still tell myself with each step, *Turn your foot in*. I have not mentioned this to anyone, not even Marise. She would probably be mortified at the fact that I still do this—no, that I still *have* to do this. But if I am to have the best shot at a long active life, I must try to preserve my hip function. So there it is: think, step, think, step.

★ ★ ★

As Rob and I forged ahead, I slowly became more active on the farm, and this in turn helped the building up of muscle and the loosening of scar tissue. That scar tissue—well, frankly, it gives you the absolute shits. After the accident, the front of my right thigh was as hard as a brick. The damaged muscle, torn by the broken femur, was so tight and painful it brings tears to my eyes to think about it.

Rob would give my thigh-deep tissue massages and work on loosening the muscle, and obviously improving blood flow to the area. This gave me relief from the pain, but as a matter of fact, it has taken seven years to get those muscles loosened up and working again. I just at this moment stood up and measured the circumference of my thighs and discovered they were similar— after my right thigh being centimetres smaller for most of those seven years. So maybe, in that respect, I have regained muscle tone.

The drought we had been drifting in and out of for the past four years now bit with a vengeance, decimating our feed and water reserves and tearing at our financial, emotional, and physical reserves as well. Once more, I was barely up to the challenge, unlike my dear wife, Marise. She once again, as she had over and over the past six years, stood strong and resilient in the face of the impending horror.

★ ★ ★

Marise and I headed off to Brisbane again on February 20, 2018, to have a check-up from Dr. King. We saw him at four in the afternoon, and he was very happy with my progress. After a chat about the journey we had shared, he shook my hand, wished me the best, and added that unless something unforeseen arose, he would not need to see me again. There was a little spring in my step as we arrived at Michelle's for our obligatory stopover, and we enjoyed her company and a few celebratory drinks.

We left Brisbane's summer heat behind us the next morning. An air of excitement and anticipation accompanied us in the car on our drive home. It was sad that our journey with Doug had come to an end. He was an extremely kind, honest, genuine person, always putting my needs and interests first and foremost.

I suppose I have an easy-going demeanour, not prone to upset people with whinging or complaining. I am comfortable going along with the natural flow of things, taking things in my stride, and placing my trust in people. It was so very easy to trust Doug; he had such a pleasant disposition and communicated in a down-to-earth, no-nonsense manner. He never spoke in complicated medical terms and was always open to questions, happily explaining things when I was in doubt or confused. I will be forever grateful for the tireless effort and wonderful job Doug did in getting me on the road to recovery—and for being a friend. I do wish him all the best in his life's journey.

★ ★ ★

Seeing the medical journey now behind us, we ventured forward towards the final stages of our journey, my ultimate recovery, and the prospect of the legal journey that hung like a dark cloud above and before us. I had maintained all along that I could handle anything the medical side of things threw at me, because everyone only had my best interests at heart. In contrast, I feared that the legal battle before us would not always have my best interests at heart but would be defined by the best storyteller and the biggest pockets. Neither gave me a warm cuddly feeling.

I was apprehensive, cautious, and afraid that we might be shafted in the forthcoming battle. I had a little knowledge of the legal ins and outs. Dad had gone through a protracted workers' compensation case years before, and I had seen how he was treated and ultimately left with little more to show for a lifetime of hard work than a few dollars and a badly damaged back. I was afraid that history was about to repeat itself, and I would end up being the unfortunate soul discarded, broken and penniless. Our prospects seemed bleak.

While the operations and such were progressing, there had been little interest or concern from the RACQ, or our legal team at Slater and Gordon, now my solicitors. But I knew things would start warming up now, as RACQ began counting its pennies and Slater and Gordon began counting mine.

9. My Piggy-in-the-Middle Legal Journey

As previously stated, I had been visited in hospital by Russell Biddle a few days postaccident and had engaged him as my solicitor in regard to the accident. I suppose initially, there was little for Russell to do, and so as things settled down and the weeks went by, I had little to no contact with him. There was an official form to be signed clarifying him as my lawyer, and that was about that. Not that this gave me any reason to be concerned. I was pretty busy doing my thing, and hospital life was fairly time-consuming and tiring. The less business, the better.

After my discharge from hospital, correspondence between Russell and I began to become more regular. I had occasional conversations with his assistants, and all was going well until about mid-2016, when we received a phone call from Paul informing us that he had just seen, on the television, a story about a Brisbane solicitor who had been charged with fraud. Lo and behold, it was Russell.

Now, Russell ran a small independent law firm, and so this seemed as if it could be the death knell for him and his business. As it turned out, he was arrested trying to leave the country for the United States and subsequently gaoled for a period of time, so there goes our solicitor. We felt a little vulnerable and very unsure as to what would happen next. Fortunately, the firm was bought out by Slater and Gordon, who were immediately in contact to assure us that my case would not suffer as a result of the takeover. The transition, as far as we were concerned, was seamless. Once we were placed in the capable hands of a new solicitor, momentum was restored, and off we went again.

One of the problems we had with the whole case was the settling of bills. I would attend an appointment, let's say for X-rays, and on completion, they would require payment. It was impossible to have the account paid by RACQ there and then, so I would pay it, and every month or so would forward all receipts to Slater and Gordon, who would forward them to RACQ for reimbursement. This was an excruciatingly painful, drawn-out process, and one that left us out of pocket to sums of hundreds of dollars time and time again.

The last couple of years, there had been no attempt by RACQ to reimburse us. In the end, we were covered by what is called *global compensation*, which at settlement covers all outstanding miscellaneous expenses incurred by the claimant and all similar future expenses. Because my claim ran on for nearly seven years, thousands of dollars were left swinging to be covered by the global section of the settlement. In the end, it wasn't easy to make sense of it all. We were also advised to keep records of all out-of-pocket expenses and voluntary work in relation to the farm, which we did, under the impression that we would be reimbursed for those expenses also. This, once again, was doubtful.

On my release from hospital in 2013, I had started doing the paperwork to access Centrelink payments to help us get through financially. I had eventually given up due to the mountain of paperwork, much of which was in relation to assets, particularly the farm. It became apparent quite soon that we would more than likely not be eligible for assistance. We had decided that we would try to get by without Centrelink support, as we would also be required to pay the moneys back upon settlement. This led to some money issues along the way, and the inability of RACQ to diligently reimburse us for medical expenses strained our resources. Still, we struggled through, telling ourselves that all would be well eventually.

★ ★ ★

The length of time the case dragged out for also meant that we went through multiple legal teams. This was another hindrance to my case, as with every change, the incoming team would have to read an ever-rising mountain of case records. We were worried that, as this team-changing continued, at times six monthly, it must be increasingly difficult for them to establish a firm grasp of the facts and issues. This proved to be the case quite often, as I would have to instruct new team members on vital aspects of the case.

I was beginning to become concerned that the quality of the case we would be able to bring to the table for settlement would be lacking in detail, and that it would be hard to ensure my legal representatives had more than a slender grasp of the intricacies of my case when settlement arrived—a thought and prospect that eventually possibly played out in our favour. Well, I hope it did.

Every time our team changed and I talked to the new leader, I would have to quiz that individual a little to assess how up-to-date the team was, and inform them of the ins and outs of my case. And my case was complicated. In most cases, the claimant has a full-time job or a paid job, and financial losses are easily calculable. In my case, being self-employed and on the farm, I had no wage, and in fact, over the few years our case ran, our income did increase, as wool and stock prices improved dramatically. So our loss could only be calculated on the loss of income we suffered because of the development work we had not been able to perform on the farm over the seven years. We then had to argue that if we had been able to do more fencing, pasture improvement, spraying, and clearing, we would have increased our productivity and our profit.

Our legal team found one other case where the claimant had indeed argued this point, but there were risks. If we chose to pursue this avenue of compensation before a judge, it would very much depend on the judge's particular interpretation of the evidence. So there was much deliberation on our side as to how we would proceed.

There would always be a pain-and-suffering component to the compensation, as well as partial disability for my leg and arm, but these would only make up a small part of the settlement. We were, as you could imagine, apprehensive about the outcome and concerned at every change along the way. More than 10 per cent of my life now had been consumed by this event, and the repercussions would impact upon us every day from here on. A positive result was essential.

★ ★ ★

Late in 2017, we drove to Brisbane to have the first face-to-face meeting with my lawyer. It was an informative meeting. The lawyer ran us through the course of events the case would more than likely follow, and he in turn found out a little more about our situation. As I said earlier, our circumstances were rather complicated, and it was only with face-to-face meetings that the intricacies of the case could be exposed. This was the meeting I referred to earlier, when the lawyer was under the impression that my condition was stable and satisfactory and we were ready to proceed to settlement.

After I informed him that there were recent CAT scans that we had no report on as yet, it was decided to put a hold on proceedings until the scans were read by Dr. King. The results of the scan confirmed that my femur was still unhealed. This led to a twelve-month wait, as it turned out, until our next meeting, which took place in early 2019.

The next meeting we attended in Brisbane was peculiar to say the least. We were informed that we were required to be in Brisbane, at the Slater and Gordon offices, early in 2019 for what we thought was another meeting with our lawyer. We were surprised and alarmed when we discovered, on arrival, that in fact we were going into mediation with RACQ. We were ill-prepared for the experience and struggled through the meeting. We came out feeling very nervous and afraid that we had done our cause little good. Mediation had broken down, and we had been cut to pieces by our lack of firm financial figures. Although the RACQ lawyer acknowledged that we had a good story to tell, he made it quite clear that firm, documented, professionally accredited reports pertaining to our financials and my physical condition were required to substantiate my case and facilitate further consideration on their part.

A despondent mood enveloped us on our journey home. The magnitude of our battle to gain reasonable compensation was becoming apparent. Our barrister, enlisted by Slater and Gordon on my behalf, had run us through the possible avenues and possibilities surrounding our way forward. There was a possibility that RACQ would not entertain the prospect of further mediation and would like to present their case before a judge. He suggested we take the initiative and file for a hearing ourselves, thus portraying confidence on our part and maybe rattling the RACQ's cage a little.

I must confess, the gamesmanship that was now taking place seemed to be overshadowing the underlying issue: namely, our future. So worry and concern once more darkened our doorstep.

The roller coaster rattled on, plunging to new depths and showing little prospect of taking a turn in our favour. There were many soul-searching moments throughout the course of our postaccident journey. The ones associated with the legal system were the darkest and least in our control.

Our barrister was quietly confident, though, that given my strong performance in mediation, the RACQ team might be reticent to proceed to court. They might possibly agree to further mediation. Both eventualities were possible. The court was also likely to order another round of mediation before hearing the case. There were many angles to get our heads around—all foreign concepts and variances far removed from our world. We felt ill-prepared to face them.

We spent many hours over the next few months going over points and discussing angles of attack we could use to firm up our case. With these tacked on to the ever-growing hardships associated with the drought, we were becoming quite frazzled and weary. We were desperate for a resolution to the whole affair, but not yet desperate enough to roll over and accept a pittance. We awaited news of further developments. We waited and waited.

Our legal team contacted us, eventually, with the suggestion that we enlist the services of a forensic accountant to do a report on the impact the accident had had on our business. The cost of this report would be significant, but they believed it was imperative we pursue this avenue of attack. They also suggested I visit an occupational therapist to evaluate my physical condition at present and access my long-term prospects.

An appointment was made with an occupational therapist. Once more we trundled off to Brisbane, this time via Lismore, where we picked up Zoe to drive us to the appointment. It was at a medical centre on the north side of Brisbane, a part of town we were unfamiliar with.

It was a typical midsummer's day in Brisbane. We arrived early, found a quaint little coffee shop just around the corner from the medical centre, and settled in for a light, nervous lunch. I was always nervous before appointments pertaining to the case. I harboured fears that my pain and limitations as a result of the accident were maybe more in my head than physical. I would manage to perform most duties on the farm in time, and so it was hard to evaluate my own disability. In fact, it was impossible. Yet the person I was now was far removed from the one who sat in that car late morning on March 31, 2013, motoring up the freeway north of Brisbane.

We sat and waited in the reception area, nervously watching the time tick by in the bottom corner of the television, set up obviously in an attempt to relieve the boredom, frustration, and nerves, of all those awaiting appointments. Eventually, a lovely young lady sought us out. She ushered Marise and I into her consultation room.

Never have I cried at a doctor's appointment. Well, I tell a little lie; once, when I had a plantar wart removed from my heel, I shed a few vainly hidden tears as I lay face down on a table while the doctor drove painkilling needles into my heal—injections he had assured me I would barely feel. I must have sensitive heels or be a wuss. More than likely the latter!

Anyway, back to the occupational therapist: I practically broke down as I retold the story of the accident, operations, daily struggles, and life postaccident. The therapist wanted to know everything I had felt, physically and mentally. She questioned Marise on many matters and, in fact, conducted the most rigorous, detailed investigation I had been through in the course of the six and a half years.

She was a lovely, caring soul who made me feel so at ease. She obviously wanted and needed me and Marise to feel comfortable enough to open up to her and give her the information she required to write her report. After quite a long talk, she assessed my physical condition, which proved to be extremely revealing, even to me. Postaccident, I had put on a few kilos of weight. The stress and inactivity had made weight gain a certainty, and this added to my physical limitations. I was now also suffering from hypertension and taking blood pressure medication to keep it in check. I was in a sorry state, though from my point of view, I was managing reasonably well.

The exercises the therapist put me through, as I said, revealed to me the true extent of my disability. Repetitive exercises were difficult to complete. I was weak and exhausted, and after about twenty minutes, I was sweating profusely and breathing heavily. I could not believe how debilitated I was. It was a sobering experience, and I left the appointment struggling to walk, my entire body tired and aching.

And so the extent of my disabilities was revealed in all its glory. The awakening to their scale was a sobering and frightening revelation. I felt like an old man. I had grown up very close to my grandparents, and Dad's father, Jimmy, had suffered for many of his last years with arthritis in all his joints. As I left the appointment that day, my movements and the pain I felt brought his condition to mind. I saw in myself an old man in body and, at that moment, spirit. The prospect of an existence in these conditions scared me.

If there was a bright side to the exercise, it came in the realisation that my condition did not exist only in my head but included real physical ailments that maybe, in time, could be improved. I spurned the idea of a lifetime of limitations as a result of these injuries. The journey so far had been one of stepping up to the mark, putting my best foot forward, and giving every challenge my best effort. I refused to drop the ball now.

My driving force had been, all along, the desire to be a lively, vibrant participant in the life before me; to enjoy my family;

work on the farm we dearly loved; and be the best friend and playmate to our grandson, Leo, and the many more we hoped were to come.

But right here and now, the focus was on the settlement and what would be required to achieve the best result possible. So although a painful realisation, the exposure of the extent, of my disability was a positive as far as our chances of success in the coming months was concerned. If the forensic accountant could reveal the full extent of financial loss we had suffered, maybe, with a little luck, we might achieve a satisfactory result, fingers crossed.

★ ★ ★

The year 2019 dragged on. The drought intensified. It was quoted as being the worst in living memory and possibly the most severe for more than a hundred years. On both accounts, we were in full agreement. Recalling Dad's memories and recollections of the 1965 drought, as far as fodder and water were concerned, we were in a far worse situation than they had been in then. The most significant difference came in the fact that we were now in our sixth year of well-below-average rainfall. The years leading up to this point had been terribly dry, and now, 2019 was far dryer than those—dryer than anyone could imagine.

Every day, we were hand-feeding all of our stock—1,300 sheep and 20 head of cattle—as well as carting water to two-thirds of them. Our days were from daylight till about five at night, when we would stagger inside to eat, shower, and try to regroup for the next day. Every week the situation worsened, and it was terrifying to imagine how much worse it could be.

As I said, we were carting water. Some we were sourcing from Bendemeer, a seventy-kilometre round trip away. Twice a week, one of us would take our little truck, with two thousand-litre shuttles on the back, into Bendemeer; bring the water home;

and pump it into other shuttles. We had hooked up water troughs in various paddocks. The availability of this water in Bendemeer was far from reliable. At times, the water point was offline, and as the drought intensified, the possibility of the water becoming unavailable was an ever-present prospect. So all in all, the situation was hand-to-mouth, day-to-day, with the only hope of relief being sufficient rain to recharge our farm dams and grow some grass. The long-term weather forecast was far from promising and proved to live up to the disappointment it promised.

★ ★ ★

In May, we were informed by our legal team that the court had ordered us to go through mediation again. The meeting was set down for August. It was impossible to tell if this was a good or a bad thing. Frankly, we had little time to ponder the situation. We battled on, day after day, week after week, in a vain attempt to crawl our way through the insidious drought. It was obviously draining us financially and emotionally. There was no doubt that it had already driven us to utter physical exhaustion.

As August rolled closer, we began to feel nervous once more—though by now, the rawness of the accident had long since been left behind. The last six and a half years had been tough, and we hoped and prayed for an end. We prayed for an end, and dreamt of a future, one without the rigours of the past years, one free of lawyers and insurance companies. Sadly, at our ages, we could not realistically hope for a future free of doctors. They would become more prevalent in our lives; of this there was no doubt. But we dreamt of a future we would be in control of, not one dictated to us by others.

Ha! I hear you say. But we were exhausted. Every time I had a call from a doctor, RACQ, or our legal team, the memories flooded back, and my mood ultimately became gloomy. I was not a happy camper. Marise did not need me when I was in these moods, honestly. She needed someone strong and resilient to help her deal with the other challenges before us.

We drove to Brisbane, hoping this would prove to be the last time we did so as a result of the accident. We arrived at Michelle's at about six in the evening, shared a cheerful dinner with her, and settled into bed, trying to sleep but failing miserably. The next morning, we plodded about the house before making our way into Brisbane central for the mediation. We grabbed a coffee, sat in the warm Brisbane winter sun, held hands, and prayed.

My God, I had prayed a lot in the last few years. Ultimately, most things had panned out reasonably well. I was even quietly confident that the drought would end soon, though I dared not mention that to Marise. But on the steps outside the Slater and Gordon offices in Anne Street that morning, we sat in silence. All that could be said had been said. The time had come, the walrus said!

10. D-Day and Beyond

We were seated in a nice sterile room—well, in the sense that it seemed devoid of anything that would constitute life, apart from us five souls: our barrister, our lawyer, the RACQ representative, Marise, and I. Proceedings were conducted in a very friendly manner. The lawyer representing RACQ was a lovely middle-aged lady whose father had been a shearer in central Queensland, and she had grown up on a farm. So our situation was certainly familiar to her.

Our barrister and this lawyer conferred to and fro for quite a while. She would leave the room and contact RACQ, return, and lay a figure on the table. They would confer again, and on and on it went. To me, there seemed little prospect of a successful resolution that day. My and our hopes were fading.

When a point of stalemate had been reached, our barrister asked if I wanted to say something. There seemed only one course of action to take. With Marise's help, I chose to give the dear lady a day-by-day account of our life on the farm in an attempt to enlighten her as to the impact my injuries and the subsequent limitations were having on not only our personal lives but our world as a whole.

I began in January and told her of every month's activities pertaining to our farm management. I wanted to enlighten her as to the pressure and the workload we were under daily, and how my condition impacted upon our world. Marise helped by adding components I missed. By the end, I was a little teary. Going through the year, point by point, had a similar effect upon me to reliving the accident. It seemed that when I went through these issues in a methodical way, the full magnitude of the event became overwhelming, and so it was today. With the drought tossed into the mix, the workload had become barely manageable. The spring period had been particularly tough. I will add that part of the dialogue as an insight into our day-to-day life:

"We lamb our ewes in the spring. Lambing begins in mid-September, with our cross-bred ewes, and continues till the end of November, when our merino ewes finish lambing. We check the ewes at about 6:00 a.m. This is necessary, as occasionally, a ewe will have trouble delivering her lamb, and if we don't assist her, she lays there with the lamb stuck in her, halfway out. If we are not there early, crows attack the lamb, chewing the lamb's tongue out, pecking out its eyes, and the ewe's eyes as well.

"The morning check takes an hour or so, if all goes well. With the drought, we then have to feed our stock, which takes about six hours, and if we have to cart water, there's another two hours. We also begin shearing in early October, which we have to do ourselves; this is because we are so busy, we cannot employ a professional shearer, who works an eight-hour day, as we do not have eight hours to attend him. So after checking ewes, feeding, and probably carting water, we would shear about forty sheep, which would take about three hours.

"After shearing and tidying up the shed, we would have dinner and an hour or so to relax before going spotlighting for foxes. Foxes come out in the night and feast upon the newborn lambs, not strong enough or fast enough to escape the hungry foxes. So we would spend a couple of hours a night spotlighting and shooting any foxes we were able to see. Foxes are also very cunning animals and become accustomed to a routine, so we have to mix up the times we go out, sometimes at about 8:00 p.m., and anytime through till 2:00 a.m. Then we get a few hours' sleep before starting all over again.

"Occasionally, we split our feeding into halves, feeding different paddocks on alternate days, but this is tough on the stock and not an ideal alternative. It is not hard to see that the demands of our farming enterprise are onerous, particularly in adverse years, and my physical condition helped little in managing the workload.

"An unfortunate consequence of all this activity surely is the negative impact it has on my body—my hips and knees. I include both right and left, because when you have a hip problem, your gait ultimately also impacts upon the other hip and knee. So as the drought continued, and the years rolled by, my condition and my long-term prognosis deteriorated. Just what I needed, but this is what we love, and I would do nothing else."

This was what I ultimately wanted to impress upon the RACQ lawyer. The farm was our life—one we chose long ago, and one we chose to maintain after the accident. It was not an easy life, and we could have walked away from it after the accident, telling ourselves that it would be unsustainable and that I would not be capable of continuing the manual workload. Still, we chose to continue on, knowing full well that if we stayed, my condition would ultimately deteriorate. That was our choice, and one we would take full responsibility for. But the accident had occurred not of our choosing and was not our fault. It had impacted upon my ability to maintain our world, my world, and there lay the culpability.

If we had chosen, through necessity, to sell our stock or even the farm because we could not manage, RACQ would never have enough money to compensate me for the loss. They would have taken my world away. How do you place a value on that?

In another aspect, I had been my own worst enemy. I had been so driven to recover from the accident, build my strength up, and regain my mobility. I had worked my arse off in an attempt to recover as well as I could and had made some impressive improvement—if only from my point of view. I could have sat on the lounge, felt sorry for myself, possibly lost all mobility, my way of life, God knows the farm, and possibly it may have ultimately become too much for Marise to manage. She might have also said enough is enough.

But I had not given up, and so once again, RACQ did not have to compensate me for any of those eventualities. I was adamant that I had done all that could have been expected of me, attended every appointment, taken numerous trips to Brisbane, even stayed with my dear sister instead of staying at motels, which would have cost RACQ much more money. We had driven to Brisbane every time, never flying, even when it was extremely uncomfortable for me to sit in a car for seven hours. We always told ourselves we were doing the right thing and not abusing the system.

So there it was, all my tale, our tale, laid before this lovely lady, in all its complexity, rawness, pain, and emotion. There was little more I could add to the narrative. I sat back in my chair with a tear in my eye and a pounding heart, after giving my all. Would it help us? God, I prayed it would!

Our barrister once again conferred with the lawyer before she once more left the room to contact RACQ and discuss where they were at. On her return, she handed our barrister a piece of paper and left again for us to discuss the offer. They were still a fair way below the figure we would have accepted or considered, and our barrister went out and talked to her again to see if there was any more movement possible on their part. She thought not but asked if we could give her twenty-four hours to talk with RACQ face to face and see what could be done. They both returned to the room, and after a chat, and her wishing us all the best, she left us to discuss our situation and our course of action from there on.

We decided to give her the twenty-four hours she had asked for instead of refusing their last offer outright. We seemed to be in a pretty strong position but didn't want to overplay our hand. We would keep as many cards up our sleeve as we could. We were still apprehensive about going before a judge, and twenty-four hours grace left both sides at the table and in the game.

★ ★ ★

It was about two in the afternoon by the time we were out of Slater and Gordon's offices, after saying farewell to our lawyer, Keiran, and our barrister. We headed for home once more. We made it to Stanthorpe just as the sun began to sink from the wintery granite-belt sky, and we decided to stay the night there.

The motel we managed to get a room at was next door to a lovely Chinese restaurant. We shouted ourselves a celebratory meal and a glass of wine on the strength of getting through what had been a tough day—and maybe finally reaching the end of our six-year ordeal. We slept well in the snug warmth of a tiny motel room on a cold winter's night. We awoke to a big frost, which made us feel at home. We had a light breakfast and headed off home.

Our thoughts were fixed on the possible outcome of the last-minute negotiations as we ventured down the very familiar New England Highway in the cool winter air beneath a crystal-clear sky. We were relieved that we had successfully negotiated the mediation the day before, and although we were still unsure as to the outcome, at least we were progressing towards an ultimate settlement and a finalisation.

We arrived home at about three in the afternoon to a cold house but the serenity of our world and our little piece of paradise.

Tomorrow, once more, the drought would be first and foremost on our minds, and the trials and tribulations of our legal battle would be resigned to a far less immediate concern. The evening was occupied with discussion about getting on top of the stock feeding tomorrow and from where we would source stock water the following week.

After another early-morning start, we were back at the house for a cuppa about ten thirty in the morning. We had no sooner sat down than the phone rang. I held my breath as our lawyer, Keiran, brought us up to date with the situation. A tense moment or two followed, until Keiran informed us that she'd had a call from the RACQ lawyer. We sat with fingers crossed.

Keiran was happy to announce that RACQ had offered $50,000 more than their final offer a couple of days earlier. That finally placed the settlement in the ballpark area we had hoped for. We instructed Keiran to accept the offer, and we were so delighted to be able to put the whole thing behind us at last. We would have to wait a couple of weeks for the money to come through, but nothing now could dampen our relief. We even let an element of excitement sweep over our world.

★ ★ ★

The settlement gave us the opportunity now to move on and take control of our lives again. I mentioned earlier that Dad had gone through a brutal workers' compensation battle years before, and for six and a half years, we had walked a similar path. During Dad's case, the insurance company had sneaked onto our farm and taken pictures, supposedly of him cutting firewood. In fact, it was a friend of ours, not Dad at all that the investigator had happily snapped. So I had been suspicious of every strange car that went up or down the road outside our place.

I had been working on our farm on and off over the six years misguidedly believing, due obviously to doctors' advice, that my leg was healed and that I should be building up to full strength again. So I would have been a prime target for some investigator's zoom lens. There had been added stress over the period, and at last, all of those dramas were relieved. In one little call, and in the blink of an eye, we were free—free to do as we pleased without the fear of a big brother watching my every move.

I had been surprised though, to say the least, that when it did come to finalising the settlement, there was no mention of my activities over the years. I had been ever honest with the doctors and physio, so there was little that was hidden from their gaze anyway.

11. Is the Sun Setting or Rising?

I sat and watched the sun rise above the tree-studded horizon. The cool spring air hung low in the valley and teased at my fingers and face. Uncertainty licked at me, tickled my mind, and danced in my thoughts.

I knew I needed to refocus and reinvent myself. My life postaccident had been consumed with doctors, physio, lawyers, exercises, and all the associated stress, which at times had been overwhelming. I had ridden a roller coaster of emotional and physical ups and downs, which had drained me of the life I'd had preaccident. I was no longer, and quite possibly would never be, the person I was before; but in all honesty, in many respects, that was not a bad thing.

Now comes the time when I must lay my cards on the table and be brutally honest with myself and you, dear reader, who has possibly found this little book a boring waste of time yet managed to remain with my ramblings to reach this gloaming chapter.

I had never considered myself a racist person, but must admit to being a guarded soul if I found myself in a crowd of people ethnically diverse from myself. I was born and raised in a very small northern New South Wales village populated predominantly by people of Anglo-Saxon heritage. My parents, most residents, and most people I knew and met in the first twenty years of my life were typically the same.

As I said earlier on, Zoe's birth and her subsequent heart condition forced me to face my own racist beliefs. I did feel ashamed of my prejudices, even though I had no dramas at all with talking and smiling to anyone who would talk or smile in return. But I knew how I felt inside, and that tore at my sense of goodness. I surely was a better person than that. Or was I?

It was not until Dad accompanied Sarah, our eldest daughter, and I to Sydney for an interview Sarah had with the department of education in Blacktown that I realised how very tolerant I was in comparison to Dad. It was the one and only time in my life that I was embarrassed by his behaviour.

Dad and I were waiting in a shopping complex while Sarah attended her interview. We sat in the food courtyard, watching and talking, as thousands of people went about their day. The disparaging comments and racist remarks Dad made—and in a voice loud enough to be heard easily by anyone near—made me feel uncomfortable, and I feared that someone would come up and take him to task. But no one did. A few just gave hollow glances as they passed. I doubt if he realised how loudly he was expressing his thoughts, and I am sure he did not mean to be heard, but the looks we were receiving revealed otherwise.

I became so conscious of the situation that I excused myself and went and browsed in a second-hand record store for a while, knowing that if I were not there, he would at least not talk out loud. Eventually the time came for us to meet Sarah, and the ordeal was over. But it had been a real eye-opener for me. Although I had always been aware of Dad's views and opinions, his public display was another thing entirely.

And so it was that at the time of the accident, I too was a little uncomfortable with the racial make-up of our society, particularly in regard to our capital cities. Even though I was embarrassed by the notion and went out of my way to prove it was not the case, the niggle still existed, barely hidden, in my subconscious. It refused all efforts to be removed.

It is said that love conquers all, and I prescribe now wholeheartedly to the theory. My prejudices stood no chance when assaulted by the love, care, and compassion shown to me by every nurse, doctor, and care worker, of every nationality, in the Princess Alexandra Hospital, and throughout my six year recovery. Every person who treated or cared for me, even the nurse who gave me a hard time in regard to the sheets on my bed and my plastered arm, only had my best interests at heart and gave their care and love freely, without exception.

Their selfless actions delivered me from my preaccident self to an improved self. I now only saw goodness in everyone I met. I now only saw wonderful people going about their daily lives, trying to get by in an increasingly difficult world. No wonder most have distant, faraway looks. Life is tough, and it must be hard to live with an eternal smile on your face and a welcoming, open heart.

I had always tried to make eye contact with people in the street and give them a smile as I passed, but now I give them a full smile. What's a full smile? Well, I can only describe it as a smile that comes from your heart—a smile that not only says "Hi" but "Have a wonderful day."

Quite often now, when I am served by a person, particularly at a supermarket checkout, I will engage them in a short conversation, asking how their day is, what they will be doing on the weekend, anything that comes to mind. Nearly all are happy to chat, and we brighten each other's day, if only for a minute or two. There are many businesses I frequent where I am greeted by a smile, and the salesperson and I will have a little chat. I know it goes beyond 99.9 per cent of all other interactions they have with customers. We don't know each other's names, just that each of us acknowledges the other's existence, and that is what it is. Basically, it is acknowledging someone else's existence.

I chatted with one lovely girl at a Woollies supermarket every time she made me a coffee. She was so bubbly and sweet in her nature, and she told me she was saving for a new car. Months later, when I enquired as to how her savings were progressing, she told me that she had decided to save for a house deposit instead. She thanked me, some months later, for the little chats we shared, adding that I was one of a very few people she had met in her three years working there who she could have a conversation with. No one else showed any interest beyond a smile and a thank you, if she was lucky.

I had been one of those people, giving little more than a smile, barely acknowledging an unknown soul's existence. Maybe there is a them-and-us mentality? Our acquaintances and friends are the *us*, and every other soul on the planet is the *them*. But we are always meeting *them* and taking them into the *us* camp. They are not foreign. We just have not as yet had the privilege of making their acquaintance! I try now to make my *us* camp include every soul on the planet. They are all prospective members, and I would hate to think that one day I passed them on the street and did not acknowledge their existence.

My reasoning may not be sound, and my beliefs possibly border on the delusional. I am judged and questioned by my own close friends. Even my dear sweet sister Michelle shakes her head often, saying, "Deanie, Deanie, Deanie" when, after a few drinks, we philosophise and ponder the world and life itself.

I know there is evil in the world; I am not entirely mad. But walking down the street, I personally find it awkward to pick out the axe murderers and rapists from the beautiful people. So I am left with a dilemma. Do I consider them all possible murderers— not likely in my case—or all wonderful, beautiful people not desiring to do anything less than live their lives peacefully without causing harm to me or any other soul? Believing as I do that that is the case, then they all deserve a smile from me and a heartfelt wish that they will live happy, full lives. I do now, quite often, when leaving a shop, thank the people who served me, wish them a good day, and also give them the blessing of a wonderful life, a blessing we all deserve.

★ ★ ★

I maintained from the beginning that I was pleased it was me who was so badly injured in the accident. I was so grateful that Marise and Paul only received minor injuries. I live with the constant regret that Sarah suffered such pain, anguish, and emotional hurt, and I will always feel responsible for that. I am so very sorry, dear Sarah. If only there was a way I could have spared you that, my sweet girl.

But I was also pleased that it was me and not any other poor person driving along the freeway that day, at that time, who was in a car hit by that vehicle, driven by that unfortunate man, who I believe never meant anyone any harm at all that day. I am not just making this up to be a martyr. I have honestly felt this way from the moment I woke in the hospital on April 1, 2013—April Fool's day. Ha ha! I really felt as if I'd been pinched and punched.

Yes, I was happy it was me. I had so much going for me, so many things in my favour, and as a family, we were well placed to battle the storm that brewed around us and forge through the tough times to come. *How could you really mean this? What in the hell's wrong with you?* I hear you ask. *No sane person thinks this way.* Well, I do.

It soon became apparent to me that I had the skills to overcome the challenges thrown at us by the accident. I was relatively young, healthy, and reasonably fit. I told everyone that I also had a weak mind, and as such had not the mental capacity to feel sorry for myself. This was not actually the truth, but it did help me to some extent to not get bogged down in negativity for too long.

Marise and I were not financially well off. In honesty, we were barely getting by. But we didn't owe any money, and with Marise's drive and determination and the help of our family and friends, particularly Dad and the girls, I was sure we would make it through. The girls had also nearly finished their secondary schooling. Zoe was halfway through year 12, which was tough on her, but she managed and made it through with a high enough ATAR to get her into university and doing an arts degree, as she had dreamed.

With Marise's hard work, we would be able to make enough money from the farm and her teaching to get by until I recovered, though none of us imagined that it would take so long. We would also be able to stay on the farm. The house was set up well enough to facilitate my needs and enable Marise to go out and work on the farm and teach with me at home alone. Though our losses over the six years were considerable, we scraped through with our marriage and family intact. A better result could not have been wished for, and we have been truly blessed.

As you can see, we were extremely lucky. Our circumstances made it possible for us to get through without any real changes to our world, and for that I will be forever grateful. I can only imagine how disastrous the same events would have been to most other families and most other people with a mortgage, young children, limited support options, and the possible mental health issues that obviously accompany such trauma. I would not wish the accident upon anyone else, ever. But as I said, I, and we, were up to the challenge, and we came out the other side relatively unscathed—and with me as a far better version of myself.

★ ★ ★

I also feel no animosity towards the driver of the other vehicle. In fact, I only feel sympathy for him, knowing in my heart that he never meant anyone harm that day, and particularly not us. I have never sat and blamed him, held him responsible, or considered him the catalyst for all my pain and our combined suffering.

Never have I thought of him as a harmful, hurtful thing, removing the real living person from his being. He will always be Jesse Hubbard, the poor soul I have never met, the man I have tried to contact over the last six years and will continue to try to contact. I need to tell him that I had forgiven him the moment I awoke in hospital. I would hate to think he lives with the thought that someone somewhere blames him for their shit life and existence.

I need him to know that I don't blame him. Our paths crossed, though we never met. Our worlds changed, as did we. I do hope he has been able to move on; get over the pain, suffering, and anguish he obviously had to deal with; and possibly, hopefully, is living a wonderful life.

★ ★ ★

After the accident, I made the same promise I think everyone makes after such an event: that I would live life to the fullest. Since I had been blessed with a second chance at life, I would not waste a minute. I must say that is true in my case. But my world has not changed much. We still live on the farm and work our arses off most days. The bills still roll in. The drought has broken, and the season at present is absolutely wonderful.

Our dear sweet girls are settled and happy. Sarah has two little boys—Leo, four and a half, and Max, one and a half; they are the joys of our life. Hannah and Jay have a lovely house and two spoilt little dogs. Zoe is thrilled after finding the person who is hopefully the man of her dreams.

My dreams have been redefined to a comfortable, serene, peaceful world surrounded by friends, family, those I love, and those who will forever hold a special place in my heart. That is all I desire. At last, my leg has healed and strengthened, and although some pain remains, I am capable of shearing a couple of days at a time without too much discomfort. I will never contemplate a return to full-time shearing. At last my mind has caught up with my body in that respect and admits the time has come to steady down.

I can still shear our sheep, though it is a steady, drawn-out process. That suits Marise and me just fine. Being able to shear makes me feel whole again. Once more, it is a part of who I am, not just who I was. I also jog a couple of times a week and find the exercise does wonders for the spirit and helps me maintain a comfortable weight.

I now find peace in the most improbable places—an inner peace that hopefully I can share with the ones I love and the world, if it only cares to partake! I see endless possibilities for humanity. Perhaps we don't have to create a new society, just tinker around the edges of the one we share. I believe we can all do better, if we only imagine we can.

★ ★ ★

The six years came and went. Would I change it if I could? Really, for me, no. I am a far improved version of myself—more thoughtful, compassionate, and tolerant. I see and appreciate the beauty around me and the beauty in everyone I know and meet. I am a happier person—not quite as crazy as before but working on it. Still a little boy, fearful and resisting the world's insistence on growing up. Maybe one day I will, but don't hold your breath. I see nothing endearing about growing up; growing old is bad enough!

For everyone else involved, yes, I would change it in the blink of an eye. The pain, suffering, and inconvenience they all went through—I would wish it all away if I could. They dealt with so much while I plodded along on my journey of recovery, mostly unable to assist them in their dramas.

Never will I have the means, words, or time to thank everyone who helped me through those years. Your love, compassion, and help has been invaluable. To those who pushed me to my limits to facilitate my recovery, those who picked me up when I fell in a heap—you all know who you are—I can only offer my deepest thanks and my eternal gratitude. Marise, you and the girls have been my guiding light, my motivation, and the reason I have remained so committed to a full recovery, to once again play an active part in your lives. You may never know what that means to me.

Not long into my journey, I realised how impossible it would be to try to recover from such an event without a family or a support network to rely on. I could see how some people crawl into a hole, never to reemerge, unable to do the physio or hard yards required to recover, finding neither will nor need to do so. Sitting on a lounge, watching television, losing their mobility and their life, watching the world pass by, and being only bystanders to their own lives. Without all the support I had, I could see that being me, and that is a sobering thought. How dependent we are on others, how important (in fact, essential) is support, and how gracious is love.

I now know happiness can be found in your normal day-to-day life. In this troubled world, you just have to open your heart, your eyes, and your mind to the beauty that surrounds your every thought, sight, and action.

I have now made the acquaintance of the better me. I am rather impressed. I hope he is proud of me and is ever mindful of how he came to be.

Printed in the United States
by Baker & Taylor Publisher Services